THE CELEBRATION OF FLESH

The

CELEBRATION

A HADDAM HOUSE BOOK

The way through the world
Is more difficult to find than the way beyond it.
WALLACE STEVENS

OF FLESH ॐ *Poetry*

in Christian Life

By ARTHUR C. McGILL

ASSOCIATION PRESS ॐ NEW YORK

Publisher's stock number: 1558
Library of Congress catalog card number: 64-18215

Printed in the United States of America

Preface

As a Protestant theologian, I have always been puzzled that within the Christian community poetry is often used for its insight into our modern miseries, but that it is rarely enjoyed as poetry. This book seeks to redress the balance. It asks whether poetry as such, without reference to the beliefs of its authors or the subject matter of its lines, whether poetry as a peculiar kind of language involving metaphor and rhythm has a significant value within the perspective of the Christian life.

I focus my attention upon three recent American poets—T. S. Eliot, Robert Frost, and Wallace Stevens. They belong to the same poetic generation, and therefore provide a microcosm of the poetry that has been available in this country in the recent past.

That I should identify poetry with the fleshly aspect of experience may seem curious, not only in view of the notoriously intellectual character of recent verse, but especially because of the spiritual emphasis in Christianity. Yet this spirituality represents a constant danger in the Christian life, if it is pursued without regard for the reality of flesh. In the kingdom of God men are created with flesh, reconciled through flesh, and glorified as flesh. To hide from the flesh for the sake of the spirit is to miss the Christian life. It is this danger that gives special meaning to the enjoyment of poetry.

Whatever enthusiasm a theologian may have for poetry and

5

poems, his thoughts and judgments must be nourished by the labor of the regular critics. The influence upon me of Owen Barfield, John Crowe Ransom, and Cleanth Brooks will be obvious to any reader who knows their works.

I especially want to thank Julian N. Hartt of Yale University for first directing me to this study. I must also express a word of my debt to the late F. O. Matthiessen. Many years ago I was aroused by his humane devotion to the language of poetry, and his disciplined insistence that poetry must be read for and through its words.

ARTHUR C. McGILL

Contents

For
LUCY

Acknowledgments

Grateful acknowledgments are due to the following publishers, authors, and other copyright holders for permission to quote poems and passages from their copyrighted works.

To Mrs. George Bambridge and the Macmillan Company of Canada Ltd., for permission to reprint a part of "The Young British Soldier" by Rudyard Kipling.

To the Clarendon Press, Oxford, for permission to reprint "A Passer-by" by Robert Bridges, from *Poetical Works of Robert Bridges*, 1936.

To Crown Publishers, Inc., for permission to reprint from *Appreciation: Painting, Poetry and Prose* by Leo Stein. Copyright 1947 by Leo Stein.

To Donald Davidson, for his kind permission to use a section of his poem "Fire on Belmont Street," from *The Tall Men*, published by the Houghton Mifflin Company. Copyright 1927, 1938 by Donald Davidson.

To Mrs. H. M. Davies and to Jonathan Cape Limited, for permission to reprint "A Greeting," from *The Complete Poems of W. H. Davies*, London, 1963.

To the Estate of Wallace Stevens and to Alfred A. Knopf, Inc., the publishers of the poetry and prose of Wallace Stevens, for their kind permission to reprint from the following editions:
The Collected Poems of Wallace Stevens, Knopf, 1954.
Opus Posthumous by Wallace Stevens, edited by Samuel French Morse, Knopf, 1957.

To Harcourt, Brace & World, Inc., for permission to reprint from

Collected Poems 1909–1962 by T. S. Eliot. Copyright, 1936, by
Harcourt, Brace & World, Inc.; © 1963, 1964 by T. S. Eliot.

To Messrs. William Heinemann Ltd., for permission to reprint "In
The Wood of Finvara," from *Poems by Arthur Symons*, published by John Lane, 1916.

To Holt, Rinehart and Winston, Inc., for permission to reprint:
The poem "Fog" by Carl Sandburg. From *Chicago Poems* by
Carl Sandburg. Copyright 1916 by Holt, Rinehart and Winston,
Inc. Copyright renewed 1944 by Carl Sandburg.
From *Complete Poems of Robert Frost*. Copyright 1916, 1921,
1923, 1928, 1930, 1934, 1939 by Holt, Rinehart and Winston,
Inc. Copyright 1936 by Robert Frost. Copyright renewed 1944,
1951, © 1956, 1962 by Robert Frost. Copyright renewed © 1964
by Lesley Frost Ballantine.

To the Houghton Mifflin Company, for permission to reprint "The
Taxi," from *The Complete Poetical Works of Amy Lowell*, 1955.

To the Literary Trustees of Rupert Brooke for permission to reprint
"Song of the Children of Heaven," from *The Poetical Works of
Rupert Brooke*, edited by Sir Geoffrey Keynes, Faber and Faber
Ltd., 1946.

To the Literary Trustees of Walter de la Mare and to the Society
of Authors as their representative, for permission to reprint the
poem "Silver," by Walter de la Mare, from his *Collected Poems,
1905–1918*, published by Henry Holt & Company, 1920.

To the Macmillan Company, for permission to reprint "The Lake
Isle of Innisfree," from *The Collected Poems of W. B. Yeats*,
Definitive Edition, 1956.

To the Society of Authors for permission to reprint a part of "Initiation" by Laurence Binyon, from his *Collected Poems*, published
by Macmillan & Co. Ltd., London, 1931.

Chapter One

The Language of Flesh

I.

DOES THE CHRISTIAN COMMUNITY have any need for poetry? The members of this community are certainly not free-floating agents, willing and able to do whatever strikes their fancies. They are determined by the special situation in which they believe they have been placed. This situation involves three elements. They are established in a special life—the divine life of God mediated to them by Jesus Christ. They are destined for a special end—the eternal enjoyment of God with Jesus Christ. They are called to a special task—the ministration of that life and joy to all men for the sake of Jesus Christ.

In view of this definite situation, poetry has often been held to be of no value, and perhaps of positive danger, for the Christian community. What have love sonnets to do with the man who knows the love of God? How can clever verses concern those who look forward to eternal life? Moreover, because poetry relishes the visible things and experiences of this world, it may distract men from the invisible promises of God. "Works of art," wrote Bernard of Clairvaux, "are idols which turn men away from God." In any ordinary collection of poems we find all the secularity and self-indulgence of which the human soul is capable. Unfortunately these works do not have a poisonous influence only on the lives of their authors. "These vipers survive their parents, and for many ages after, like epidemic diseases, infect whole generations, corrupting and unhallowing the best-gifted souls, for whose sanctification and welfare the

Son of God laid down his life." So said Henry Vaughan in 1655. In this perspective, it is often judged to be the better part of wisdom for the Christian to avoid poetry, and to seek more edifying discourse.

Just the opposite view, however, has been prevalent in the English-speaking world during the last two centuries. Poetry and the Christian community have found themselves united in a common opposition to the cold ruthlessness of science. The scientific spirit was thought to deny the validity of imaginative insight on the one side and of religious faith on the other. For a while its denial seemed to carry the day, and poets and Christians shared a kind of fellowship of defeat. In recent years, however, the situation has been reversed. Scientific realism has lost its glow of unlimited promise. In many areas it is viewed with suspicion. Poetry and Christianity have now become aggressive, joining together in a severe analysis of "the human predicament" and executing a broad critique of our "contemporary situation." One hundred years ago Christians read Wordsworth and Tennyson to reassure themselves about human values in a climate of scientific materialism. Today they read Eliot and Auden to understand the deep spiritual crisis to which that materialism has brought them. Poems, it is widely believed, may give the Christian community insight into the spiritual conditions of our day. Armed with this knowledge, Christians are in a better position to serve the real needs of others and to advance the name of Christ.

It is obvious that both the older suspicion and the more recent approval of poetry have been largely determined by considerations of subject matter. Those who find verse trivial, if not dangerous, protest that it does not speak directly of God or of his work in Christ. It dwells on the chaos of feeling and fancy that mark life in this world. Those who see the Christian relevance of poetry emphasize the general picture it gives of the human situation. A poem, they claim, may show the triumphant vivacity of man's spirit over the material universe, or it may show the misery of life in a Godless world.

When poetry is assessed in any of these ways, however, it is easily misunderstood. For no poem exists merely to serve some general subject matter. It does not and cannot simply advance religion or express a viewpoint or diagnose a suffering. It comes into being as an *experiment with words*. It is an effort to mold the stubborn material of language, so that it will articulate perceptions and take on forms that otherwise it does not have. A poem cannot be understood until it is first enjoyed, and enjoyed because of its poetry—because of the images and rhythms of its language—and not for any other reason. This is the first law, so to speak, in the reading of any verse. If you are not charmed or intrigued by the words of a poem, you will not really understand it in any of its other aspects. But if it does delight you, then you have already understood it, at least at its most important level. You have "stood under" and been gripped by the spell of its language.

The attitudes toward poetry among Christians have usually not been concerned with the fact of poetic language. Poems have not been read as works to be enjoyed, but as tools for heightening a man's consciousness of God, or for eroding his confidence in the secular world. In either case, no value has been given to their literary qualities.

To correct this oversight, we must clear away two widespread notions.

1. We must completely dispel the impression that a writer uses his poetry to express his view of the world, that is, to record the values and beliefs and principles which he personally has found meaningful in life. Poetry is simply not the proper language for exhibiting and validating a world-view. Its images and rhythms do not contribute to the kind of clarity and cohesion needed for this. On the contrary, it is really preoccupied with quite a different level of experience. This level is far removed from the question of a "world-view." As we shall see, it requires the peculiar techniques of rhythm and imagery to become verbally articulated. Hence there is no point for a Christian to try to assess a poem by its conformity to Christian doctrine. It does not present itself simply as a statement of its author's convic-

tions, and therefore readers cannot adequately handle it simply in terms of their own self-conscious beliefs.

2. We must also dispel the notion that the Christian life is primarily a matter of believing certain general ideas. We often read books that sketch such a "viewpoint Christianity," and contrast the Christian "position" on some matter with the positions of humanism, say, or naturalism or Marxism. But the actual life of the Christian community cannot be portrayed in such terms. "Faith" is not the possession of a settled world-view, which people can interpose between themselves and the shock of experience, and by which therefore they can keep the world at an arm's length away from them, can solve all their problems, and can arrange themeslves with the "right" attitudes for every situation. On the contrary, "faith" has the effect of *opening* a man to the world, to his neighbors, and to himself. It deprives him of all self-conscious postures. It propels him into a living engagement with concrete experience.

These questions of poetry on the one hand and of the Christian life on the other must now be examined in detail.

II.

The decisive feature of poetic language is its sensuousness. A poem does not take an abstract view of things, and it does not express the attitudes of a free-floating consciousness. It focuses upon the dynamic interaction between a man's mind and some bit of the world that flows in upon his senses. Here are some brief passages, where concrete experience figures in a variety of ways.

> I saw Eternity the other night
> Like a great *Ring* of pure and endless light,
>   All calm as it was bright;
> And round beneath it, time in hours, days, years,
>   Driv'n by the spheres,
> Like a vast shadow mov'd, in which the world
>   And all her train were hurl'd.
>   *Henry Vaughan, 1655*

When you're wounded and left on Afghanistan's plains,
And the women come out to cut up what remains,
Jest roll on your rifle and blow out your brains
An' go to your Gawd like a soldier.
> *Rudyard Kipling, 1892*

And like a dying lady, lean and pale,
Who totters forth, wrapped in a gauzy veil,
Out of her chamber, led by the insane
And feeble wanderings of her fading brain,
The moon arose up in the murky East,
A white and shapeless mass—
> *Percy Bysshe Shelley, 1820*

When I go away from you
The world beats dead
Like a slackened drum.
> *Amy Lowell, 1914*

Behold the child, by Nature's kindly law,
Pleas'd with a rattle, tickled with a straw.
Some livelier play-thing gives his youth delight,
A little louder but as empty quite.
Scarfs, garters, gold amuse his riper stage;
And beads and pray'r-books are the toys of age.
Pleas'd with this bauble still, as that before;
Till tir'd he sleeps, and Life's poor play is o're.
> *Alexander Pope, 1733*

Needles and pins, needles and pins,
When a man marries his trouble begins.
> *Nursery rhyme*

He was a worthy citizen of the town.
"Where is the fire?" he babbled as he ran.
"The fire! The fire!" spat between pursy breaths.
He dropped his question, stuck his gross right hand
Against his watch-chain, ran, and stared, and sobbed,
Out Belmont Street? My God, that's where I live!

Stumbling with slow fat feet and tragic breath
While roaring sirens passed upon the wind.
                                    Donald Davidson, 1927

In all these examples, the reader finds his imagination engaged in something palpable and concrete. The language does not allow him to think about eternity or the waning moon in a vague general way. It wants him to comprehend—or better, to sense—these things as ingredients of his perceptual experience, as things that disclose themselves to him through his senses. "I *saw* Eternity the other night." In Vaughan's lines eternity never becomes an abstract idea, to be defined by the negation of another abstract idea, time. It is apprehended solely through the contrast between light and darkness. Similarly the nursery rhyme and the passage by Pope do not try to infer the general conditions of human life from a number of facts. By an act of immediate insight, the mind is presented with these general conditions in and through some concrete details—through the needles and pins in the one case, through the noisy rattle in the other.

All poetry has this sensuous dimension. It always presents its subject matter in terms of "images." An image is any representation of sensory experience in words. Shelley's description of the sick old lady is an image. So are the lines that present us with the slackened drum, or with the man running and panting for breath, or with the Afghanistan women "cutting up what remains" of the wounded soldiers. Sometimes the concrete object that is imaged in words has itself a further meaning. Shelley's sick old lady, for instance, is really the moon. But often the concrete is actualized simply for its own sake, as something charming or vivacious in itself. In any case poetry is primarily a language of images. It expresses what men see and think and feel when their senses are alive, and their whole consciousness is working through what they perceive. "It always endeavors to arrest you," T. E. Hulme said, "and to make you continuously see a physical thing, to prevent you from gliding through an abstract process." [1] There has long been the view that a poem is simply a speaking picture.

The passages given above do not consist of images only. They also involve a vibrant human response. They show a mind reacting to the concrete situation, a mind alive with unexpected feelings and insights. This responsiveness is conveyed primarily through the *style*. Style is not simply an aspect of the words, something an author adds to his composition to make it sound pretty, after he has written down what he wants to say. Style is primarily the expression of the *attitude* in the responding mind. Kipling's verse on the soldier is vibrant with bitterness; Shelley's reflects an undertone of disgust; Vaughan's is pervaded by a feeling of tranquility, and Davidson's by a feeling of panic. A poem is always a voice speaking, like that of a character in a play. The tone of that voice—that is, the style—is where the responding mind presents itself. A poet need not rely just on this tone of voice. He may name and describe the response in so many words.

> The night sky billowed with gold
> And I felt such joy as only shepherds know.

Often, however, poets avoid this kind of explicitness. They prefer to let the responding consciousness become so vibrantly present in the tone of voice that there is no need to name or describe the feelings.

Having identified these two conspicuous elements in poetry—a concrete situation and a vibrant human response—we now must look at their interaction. And this brings us to the really decisive point. For in poetry the connection between these is direct and immediate. The language does not raise questions about whether things are as they appear. It shows the world and the responding consciousness in a relationship of *open engagement*. But why does poetry do this? Because this represents an actual and continuing condition in every man's experience of the world, and because poetry wants to express or recover what the mind is aware of in this condition.

The aspect of experience involved here is the moment of *immediate contact*, when some item in the environment—an object, a movement, a situation—dynamically imposes itself upon a man, and grips his attention. He sees that the moon has a sick and ugly appearance. In the child's playing with a rattle, he suddenly experiences that fatuity of all human life. Some house on his own street is on fire. He has not planned or arranged to perceive these things. Because of some striking quality in them, they have seized his attention in spite of himself, and interrupted whatever dreams or projects he may have been pursuing.

In this condition, as it is actually experienced, a man is not aware of himself as one thing and the world "outside" as something else. Some concrete reality flows into his mind, and arouses, as if by its own creation, a whole constellation of emotional, imaginative, and intellectual responses. These do not yet belong to "me," as if "I" were a special domain, clearly and neatly closed off from everything else. The mind has not yet drawn in upon itself, to look back upon whatever confronts it from across a distance. These feelings and associations and ideas are still continuous with the world that provokes them. "I" seems simply to be the place where they are brought forth.

On the other hand, the self in this moment of immediate contact reaches out and grips what comes to it. It does not throw interpretations at the world. The objects and events that it encounters seem to be actualizations of its own emotions and thoughts. Starlight seen a certain way brings an awareness of eternity into focus. For a departed lover, the world as actually experienced does go dead like a slackened drum. As long as this condition lasts, things do not retreat into that closed, self-contained "world" out there. They are still in immediate continuity with the human mind.

This is the level or condition of experience that poetry tries to articulate. In the images of a poem we recover a sense of how reality is when it makes an immediate perceptual impact upon the consciousness. In a poem's style or tone of voice, we recover a sense of how the living consciousness is when it vitally responds to this immediate impact.

We must make one further observation: this whole engaged level of experience occurs through the medium of a man's senses, that is, through his flesh. There the actual world flows in upon him, and there every level of his consciousness moves into contact with the actual world. It is in this sense that I speak of poetry as "the language of flesh."

The use of this term "flesh" must be carefully explained. It is not being used to designate man's physical appetites, which may break out of control and corrupt his life with lust. This degenerate moral state is usually contrasted with the state of self-control, where the disengaged, self-conscious ego is master of everything in its own household. For those who are drawn by the example of Jesus Christ, this state of self-control seems just as perverse and corrupt as the state of unrestrained sensuality. It is no better to let the vitality of the ego enslave the appetites than it is to let the vitality of the appetites enslave the ego. The shadow of death embraces them both alike, so that men do not find life simply by freeing one of these from all restraint. Life lies outside of them both.

At the same time, "flesh" is not used here to mean the organic body of a man, in separation from his withdrawn and disengaged mind. The word sometimes designates that aspect of him which belongs to nature, his physiological processes, the chemical or electrical reactions which make up his sensations, the carcass that remains after he dies.

Both of these uses of the term carry the same general meaning: flesh is what is left of us when our minds are taken away. On the subjective side, this leaves our appetites. On the objective side it leaves our bodies. But why should our bodily dimension be contrasted with and made external to our minds? For that is not at all the case in those moments of immediate experience, when something grips and holds our attention. Then our flesh is not felt to be something outside of our conscious selves. On the contrary, it is a *perfectly transparent medium*. Our minds look through it—or, better, pass through it—effortlessly to reach a concrete situation. Or we might say, the concrete situation passes through it to grip our minds. Here the term "flesh" is not part of the artificial effort to make man into an object and then to label his parts. Man must be considered as a dynamic experiencer, and in that context his flesh appears to him as a medium through which he meets the world. Far from being alien to his mind, it is the source of its life. It nourishes his whole consciousness by placing him in vital relationship with the real.

Poetry is the language of flesh in this sense. It finds words to crystallize the state of immediate impact, when the responsive mind and a bit of the world are dynamically engaged. A poem may focus on a single moment, in an effort to realize the full intensity of impact and response. Short lyrical poems, like Shelley's sketch of the waning moon, have this character. Or a poem may follow some incident, like the fire on Belmont Street, or a chain of incidents, like the *Odyssey*, not in order to report these from the outside, in the manner of a historical account, but to bring out what they are like from the inside to someone living through them. Again a poem may explore an idea or moral truth, not insofar as this belongs to the realm of abstract thought, but insofar as it is apprehended in and through the concrete. There is no limit to the range and variety of poetry. It all, however, has an orientation toward the condition of immediate experience.

That is why we cannot identify it simply with the feelings that it expresses, and call it a language of human emotions. Then we would be ignoring its images, its power to convey the immediate impact of things. Neither can we identify it solely with the concrete world that it presents. This would ignore the human responsiveness that it voices in its style. Poetry is a significant mode of speech precisely because it does not require either the self or the world to stand by itself. It explores the dimension of experience where these two poles are completely engaged with each other and have not yet broken apart.

III.

In giving such emphasis to the immediate impact of experience, we must not lose sight of the problems of poetic composition. Having an immediate experience does not automatically give a man the language to articulate it in words. On the contrary, ordinary language is remarkably unqualified for this purpose. It has the effect of suppressing the immediacy of things and of presenting them from the viewpoint of routine common sense. It stresses what is public and obvious. Therefore we have to say that while a poet seeks to recover experience at its most primitive level of openness and engagement, he himself in his conscious mind begins at the other extreme. His deliberate awareness is wholly molded by everyday speech. Normally he thinks and talks, not of things in their concrete impact, but in terms of the rather diluted and public aspect of the world that we find preserved in the rough and ready language of the street.

Beginning at this public level, the poet must work his way back toward an awareness of immediate experience. He must break free from the perspectives of ordinary speech. He must put his sentences in peculiar forms, so as to catch the sting of things in their immediacy. He must become *detached*, not from the concrete world as such, but from that world as he knows it through his normal habits of consciousness.

In order to understand the discipline and detachment involved in writing a poem, we may reflect more closely on the problems of ordinary speech. After all, people in everyday life are constantly trying to convey the immediate impact of their experience—whenever they describe a scene or tell about a trip or characterize one of their friends. Think of the tired commuter who comes home in the evening to tell his wife about the dreary day he has had at the office, about his secretary's blunders and Anderson's temper, about the mix-up in the memos and the disagreeable lunch, about the report that has to be done over and the traffic jam coming home. This man is trying to convey the concrete impact of things and to register his own vibrant response. Why is it necessary to bother with poetry? Why have stanzas? Why have figures of speech?

But consider our tired commuter. What happens after he completes this oppressive catalogue of frustrations? Has he succeeded in giving his wife a vivid sense of his day? Unfortunately he has not. In fact, in his words she has heard only his exasperated temper. She decides that he wants to be left alone, and so retires with the children to another room. Instead of actualizing his day for her, he has only frightened her away. Nor do others have much better success when they describe a trip or try to give a word-picture of one of their neighbors. These people do not realize the enormous difficulties involved in getting words to perform this function. They take as natural what can be achieved only by laborious discipline. We may consider four of these difficulties.

1. In the first place most men never really notice the way in which things strike them in the moment of immediate experience. They are caught up in their various preoccupations. They have their minds focused on some task or some problem. The objects and situations close at hand pass by unnoticed. This evasion is reinforced by familiarity. Every day they encounter the same faces, pass through the same places, make use of the same things. They take the concrete world for granted, and no longer bother to notice it. They are in a state of partial anesthesia. They have to go abroad to find a fresh and unfamiliar world, but their evasion of immediate experience has by now become so habitual that they no longer know how to focus on what directly confronts them, even when they want to. Not the least source of trouble here is their lopsided reliance on their eyes. Vision has a way of putting things at a distance, and making them seem remote and stale. People tend to become oblivious of all their other senses. They forget that in any given moment what they hear or smell or touch may have a more gripping effect upon them than what they see.

All this means only that most people do not develop the art of concentration on their perceptual experience, do not open themselves fully and deliberately to the impact of a rose or a room. They do not let their consciousness approach anything closely enough, or respond to it richly enough, or stay with it long enough, or relish it with enough of their senses to appreciate its actual impact. When they go to tell someone else about it, they have nothing appropriate to say.

Here, then, is the first discipline required of the poet. He must learn to concentrate his attention on the immediate impact of things. He must not let his preoccupations distract him from his perceptions. He must be less concerned with trying to change a situation than is the ordinary man, and more willing just to experience it as it is. He must *notice* things. He must keep on noticing things, and must do so with all his five senses. He must be aware of the smell and touch of objects, as well as of their visible appearance. If the poet is able by words to recover a sense of the rich impact of things, it is because he has trained himself to be richly aware of them.

2. A different problem is posed by the fact that things appear quite differently in the dynamic thrust of immediate experience than they do as neutral objects. For when they first seize our attention, we are not clear about their objective identities. A car coming toward us out of the shadows may on the first instance seem like a bird. In fact it may be a bird as far as our vibrant response is concerned. Immediate experience is not a realm of settled identities. It is a realm of *metamorphosis*. An individual item may seem first one thing and then another. This kind of confusion is not due to any weakness in our eyesight. It arises because we can know the settled identity of something only by mentally stepping away from it, exploring it systematically to test its character, getting rid of deceptive shadows or confusing resemblances, looking at it in its total setting and total behavior. But in the moment of immediate experience our minds are not involved in any of these activities. A something suddenly confronts us and awakens a number of remnants out of our experience. We are startled by the sound of the wind on the windowpane, and for an instant we are reliving an old experience, and are again on that ocean liner during the storm. The swerving form of the car makes it seem exactly like a bird. Immediate experience is drenched with this uncertainty, this metamorphosis in which one thing or situation turns into another and as quickly turns back again.

The mind is not deceived. It does not forget the real objective thing that confronts it. At the same time the power of the first impression gives this other, similar thing a momentary actuality that cannot be denied. As long as the mind is responsive to concrete experience, it can only recognize this doubleness, this shift of identity that keeps occurring. The deeper influence of things upon us is often related, not to their objective identity at all, but to their strange way of becoming something else in the thrust of immediate experience, to their power of metamorphosis.

In recovering the impact of immediacy, it is not enough for a man to report what has been encountered. He must free his language from the inert world of settled identities. He must escape from the power of names. He must show the event of metamorphosis, in which one thing seems in its vibrant presence to become something else. This requires him to develop and discipline his *imagination*.

The imagination does not simply concoct fanciful fictions and make up unreal situations. It is the organ that grasps the resemblances between separated things, and thus enables the mind not to be frozen to the objective situation that surrounds it. The imaginative power is able to *see* one thing as if it actually were something else, so that a car moving from the shadows does not strike us always as a dull, ordinary, and familiar car, and the waning moon is not always and only just that remote astronomical body. The imagination is constantly working in every mind, and is particularly active at the level of immediate experience. A man's response to the impact of things in the first moment is always primarily imaginative, always aroused to see things not only for what they are objectively, but also for the other things which they resemble and can turn into.

In the case of our tired commuter, as long as he describes the disagreeable items from his day in their static identity, and ignores the metamorphic changes that were a crucial part of their impact upon him, he will not convey what he encountered. He will leave unspoken the imaginative dimension of his own response. The unpleasantness of lunch amounted to "cold potatoes," as if this objective fact could explain anything. He relies on the power of names. As a result, his day will seem like a static, flat, two-dimensional scene, with no echoes of the other places and other situations that it kept triggering in his mind, with no hint of the many dimensions of exasperated experience through which he was actually passing.

The poet is the man who fully recognizes the imaginative aspect of immediate experience. He takes care to present the metamorphic changes involved. For this purpose he develops *metaphors*. A metaphor is a statement in which one thing is presented in terms of another, as Shelley, for instance, in the lines given above, presents the moon as a sick old lady. The essence of the metaphor, however, is that it does not offer merely a comparison between two static things, both of which stand forth in their own right and have their points of similarity duly noted. In a metaphor, it is made clear to the reading imagination that only one and not two objects are involved, but that this one entity is being apprehended in two different ways, as if it were changing from being one thing to being another.

In Shelley's passage, we know that there are not two items in the actual situation, a moon and a woman, and therefore we are not prompted to go through the mental process of making a comparison. It is rather as if the same object, without any alteration in its appearances, changes its nature. What impresses itself upon us as an old woman in the first lines suddenly becomes the moon. In other words, a metaphor gives us the experience of a metamorphosis. Its power depends on how completely the one dissolves into the other, on how effectively the same immediate data—paleness of color, blankness of expression, indistinctiveness of detail—can be made to grip our minds as both a woman and the moon with equal plausibility.

Here is a metaphor by W. H. Davies that does not achieve this doubleness.

> My pockets nothing hold,
> But he that owns the gold,
> The Sun, is my great friend—
> His spending has no end.

The point of these lines is clear enough. The sun's bright radi-

ance is presented as a gracious disbursal of gold to someone
with empty pockets. But there is no dynamic interaction here,
no imaginative experience of transformation. Before our minds
the sun in its immediate presence does not turn into a spender.
The two components remain external to each other. One belongs to the realm of actual experience, but the other seems to
exist only in the poet's fancy. It has not been made part of perceptual reality. Compare with this the following metaphor by
Shelley.

> My soul is an enchanted boat,
> Which, like a sleeping swan, doth float
> Upon the silver waves of they sweet singing.

We know that in fact this person is listening to a voice. But the
double image of the boat and the swan so effectively crystallizes
the qualities of this experience that we also have a sense that the
person actually *is* floating in peaceful sleep upon a river.

Metaphor is crucial to all poetry. It serves to break up the
static and objective character which things have when they are
considered from a distance and securely identified. It frees the
mind from the illusion of names. It recalls it to that realm of
immediate experience where nothing is just itself but keeps turning into other things, where every moment is alive with objectively impossible possibilities. For an instant a tree becomes
an elephant, a car becomes a bird, the dead leaves on a winter
beech tree become the rich luxuriant blossoms of May. Of
course, the ordinary man avoids this level of his experience. It
threatens all the logic of his practical life. How can he get on
with the tasks at hand if he keeps noticing that the moon becomes a veiled and sick old lady? But this is the level that interests the poet, and that his disciplined imagination tries to
recover with metaphors.

3. When the ordinary person wants to convey the actual impact of things, the chances are that he shows a whole range of
un-co-ordinated attitudes. And this means that he speaks in a
babel of different and even contradictory styles. To return to the
tired commuter again, he thinks that his feelings about his day

are simple and easily expressed. He does not realize what a variety of emotions he betrays in his speaking voice—self-pity over his own unhappiness, exasperation at others, shame and perplexity that he has not made the day a success. As he speaks, each of these feelings keeps appearing and then disappearing. Each involves a tone of voice—a style—which does not last long enough to make an impression. In this mass of shifting emotions, nothing stands out clearly but the man's personal irritability.

This problem also is one that the poet must overcome. He cannot let his poem be a confusion of attitudes. The responses expressed there must be selected and co-ordinated. They must have a coherence much greater than is found in real life. This means that a poet cannot write his poems directly out of his own actual experiences. His reactions as a man to real situations are too complex and too confused to allow a unified attitude to emerge spontaneously. He can create a poem only in the seclusion of his study, where there are no real events to crowd him with new feelings, and where he can select and control the responses that his words will express.

Even more important, he must develop an ear for tones of voice, for the emotional nuance that is carried by the sound of a phrase or by the rhythm of a sentence. "Ascending" and "soaring," for instance, may be synonyms, but they lend themselves to the expression of quite different emotional possibilities. The poet must learn to catch how a single word can alter the whole rhythmic impact of a line, and thus give an entirely new tone to the voice that speaks it. Wallace Stevens describes this side of a poet's work.

> You can compose poetry in whatever form you like. . . .
> It is not that nobody cares. It matters immensely. The slightest sound matters. The most momentary rhythm matters. You can do as you please, yet everything matters.
> . . . You have somehow to know the sound that is the exact sound; and you do in fact know, without knowing how.[2]

To write ten lines that have a real and yet unified tone in-

volves the poet in a long process of trial and error. He must
experiment with different words and explore different breathing
patterns in the sentence structure. And when the lines are completed, it is no longer possible to identify the attitude they express with the real-life attitudes of the man who wrote them.
Undoubtedly there is some connection, but it need not be as
direct as many people believe. For in his work he has not simply
given expression to his own feelings. He is more like a dramatist
creating an imaginative character. The tone of voice and attitude that finally emerge in the lines do not arise directly from
his own experiences, but from his working again and again over
the words, picking up and exploring the emotional overtones in
this phrase, discarding the tone of voice in that rhyme, until at
last his ear is satisfied that emotional coherence has been attained. By that time his lines may be voicing an attitude quite
removed from his own real-life personality.

4. When men normally speak to each other, they are inatten-
tive, not only to what they encounter and to the confusion in
their own feelings, but also to their language. They assume that
words will automatically express the feel of things in the moment of immediate impact. They rely on standardized phrases
that could be used equally well in a thousand other contexts.
They pile up vague expressions, without pausing to test or
choose their words. As a result, their statements convey the
obvious and conventional level of experience, but nothing of the
vibrant shock of the concrete.

This is the fourth difficulty that the poet must overcome:
taking our crude daily speech and making it succeed where it
usually fails. He can do this because ordinary language, behind
the routine way it is often used, actually does participate in the
kind of immediate experience that concerns poetry.

We often think of words as counters to which men assign a
certain meaning and which for the rest of their existence signify
that meaning whenever they are used. But this is not true. Words
are not only tools of the withdrawn mind, which observes the
world from a distance and has everything neatly catalogued under clear labels. Words arise when men are absorbed in the

thrust of concrete immediacy, and therefore carry with them the richness and emotional intensity of such encounters. Everything that we meet in our immediate experience is enmeshed with a profound human response. When in that moment we name it with a word, that word not only denotes the object, but also evokes a sense of the object in its vibrant immediacy and conveys the whole cluster of responses associated with it. Try to use the word "Buchenwald" as a merely geographic term, or "assembly line" in a purely neutral way.

This part of the meaning of a word is not given to it by a deliberate act of will. This it acquires simply by usage, by repeatedly appearing in connection with certain immediate experiences. This part of its meaning cannot be given to it by any individual person, but only by the practice of a whole community over a long period of time. It certainly cannot be given in a dictionary definition. This part of its meaning also undergoes slow but constant change. We forget that the words we use every day on the telephone have had a long history, and have been associated with the immediate experience of living men for many centuries. These past associations do not suddenly vanish from a word, as if by the fiat of some scholarly committee. They continue to cling to it, in however soft an undertone. Therefore even if a person never went to school and never learned a single fact of history, he would yet be meeting and sharing in the whole historical experience of his community through his language. Living speech at any time carries within itself the immediate feel of things as known to previous generations. Every word, then, has a depth and richness far beyond what is recognized by the objective mind and recorded in the dictionary. It has a kind of vital life of its own, a power to call to mind a set of associations, an atmosphere of concrete encounter and response.

This depth and richness in a word is what the poet depends on, in order to make daily speech succeed, as the language of fleshly experience. He trains his ear to listen to the way words are used, hearing their present life in conversation and their past life in books. Then he spends his hours with pencil and paper, finding just the right combination and arrangement of words, just

the right rhythms and rhymes, to bring out the full weight of
the immediate experience that vibrates in them. In all these
poetic devices, however, he himself puts nothing new into daily
speech, any more than the sculptor puts something new into his
stone. By means of the form that he gives it in his verse, he
simply draws out the life present but up to now hidden within it.

IV.

These are some of the difficulties that prevent people from
expressing the impact of immediate experience. The world at
that level sweeps in upon them too swiftly and too richly, and is
too fully alive with transformations to be presented by any casual statement. It can be caught and held only by a form of words
that has been carefully prepared, a form mobile enough not to
give things a false stability, and yet unified enough not to dis-
sipate them in a vague confusion. This form is what the poet
makes for us. By disciplining his attention, his imagination, his
emotions, and above all his ear for language, he learns how to
realize the flash and sting of immediacy.

People enjoy the words of a poem because of this flash and
sting, because the waning moon or the fire on Belmont Street or
the ugliness of war is actualized concretely. For most men, life
is a perpetual evasion of the here and now. They are always turning their attention away from their fleshly experience, in which
the world keeps shocking and exciting them. They never notice
the things and faces and places that flow in upon their minds.
They rush to the store without realizing how the sheen of light
on the river has lifted their spirits. They chat with a person
without recognizing how much the stoop of his shoulders has
disturbed them. They do not live on the surface of their skins.
They keep moving away from the present instant into various
preoccupations.

The result is inevitable: a person soon comes to believe that
things in immediate experience have no substance of their own.
They dissolve away too easily before his mental conceptions.

They prove interesting only after his rational mind has interpreted them or after his ambitious will has made use of them. As far as he is concerned, immediate experience is nothing but "mere sensation."

In works of poetry, this person finds himself drawn away from this half-real world. The moon stands forth as something new and fresh, as something that grips him with its own unmanageable intensity, and that arouses in him, not "mere sensation," but responses at every imaginative and intellectual level of his consciousness. Poetry shows him that concrete experience, far from being a springboard from which his mind must soar away, is itself the promised land. Poetry restores him to the richness of immediate reality. As Wallace Stevens notes, "Its function, the need which it meets and which has to be met in every age that is not to become decadent or barbarous is precisely this contact with reality as it impinges on us from the outside, the sense that we can touch and feel a solid reality which does not wholly dissolve itself into the conceptions of our own minds." [3]

In this sense I speak of poetry as the *celebration* of flesh, the celebration of the actuality and richness of our fleshly engagement with the world. Not that everything encountered here is pleasant and reassuring; quite the contrary. But everything is encountered in a rich *way*. It is present with its own vital dynamism, and not as an illustration for some world-view or as a dull item of common sense. It surges forward with its own authenticity and does not require explanations. Against all evasions and withdrawals, poetry celebrates this fleshly mode of experience. Even if great anguish is expressed here, it is at least the anguish of a voice engaged with the concrete.

V.

With this sketch of the poet as one who celebrates concrete experience, we can better understand the suspicion with which poetry has often been viewed in the Christian community.

The suspicion arises from a false other-worldliness. Because the Christian life seeks its fulfillment wholly and solely in God, it is sometimes concluded that the Christian must avoid or anesthetize all contact that he has with this world. Are we not told that Christ came to deliver us from "this present evil world"? (Gal. 1:4.) Does not Paul warn us to "make no provision for the flesh" and to "put to death the deeds of the body"? (Rom. 8:13; 13:14.) Does not Christ lead the way into a rigorous asceticism, in which all earthly joys are renounced for the sake of heavenly beatitude? Does not our love for God disentangle our souls from all affection for creaturely things? "When I love thee, what do I love?" Augustine asks. "*Not* the beauty of any body, *not* the order of time, *not* the clearness of this light which so delights my eye, *not* the harmony of sweet songs of every kind, *not* the fragrance of flowers or spices, *not* manna nor honey nor limbs that enjoy the embrace of physical love. These things I do not love when I love my God." [4] That is why, according to some, a person can properly love God only by escaping from this fleshly world, and by turning his back on that whole level of concrete experience which poetry celebrates. Unless he does this, his love will continue to feed on mammon. He will be like the rich young man who would not sell all that he had and follow Jesus, even for the sake of eternal life.

The great difficulty with this kind of spiritualistic Christianity is that it confuses the "what" with the "where" of Christian love. *What* men love when they share in the divine life is God alone, with all their mind and soul and strength. If their love touches anything else, it does so only in obedience to Him. However, *where* they are when they love God is not in some pious ivory tower. They are in the world, not withdrawn from it. They are men of flesh and sensory perception, immersed in the concrete physical actualities of their surroundings and subjected to the concrete physical sufferings of their race. It was as flesh that God came to them in Jesus Christ and extended His life to them. It is through the physical movement of human tongues and the physical sound of human voices that He continues to disclose himself to them. It is through bread and wine—the very things that increase and support the substance of their flesh—

that He continually nourishes them with the body and blood of His Son. It is for the mutual support of their fleshly needs that He commands them to serve each other—not with spiritual gymnastics or excessive achievements of piety, but with food and shelter, with the clothing from their own bodies and with the physical life-blood from their own veins. Men no more meet each other as spirits in the Christian church than anywhere else. Their concrete bodies are always the place and the medium for their life together, as well as for their life with God. Your body is the temple of the Holy Spirit. (I Cor. 6:19.) The life you live by faith in Christ is the life you now live in the flesh. (Gal. 2:20.) You never hate your own flesh, but you nourish it and cherish it, just as Christ does his church. (Eph. 5:29.)

It is not the case that the Christian life locates people in some spiritual elsewhere. The "new man," whom God brings forth in a person, according to the New Testament, is not himself spirit. He is flesh that *has* God's spirit, or that is *in* God's spirit. And he is flesh not only now, but also in the final state of beatitude toward which he moves. His blessedness will involve, not the removal, but the resurrection and glorification of his body. His heavenly existence will not be ethereal, but will be just as much enmeshed in a concrete world as is his present life. That world, however, will be different in character, since it will be covered everywhere with the splendor of God's glory. The "world" and the "flesh" that the New Testament constantly warns against do not refer to the concrete life as such, but to the concrete life that has become closed in upon itself and that lives in rebellious independence of God.

The New Testament keeps two points always yoked together, without letting either compromise the other. Men find their life in God alone, as He gives himself to them in Jesus Christ, but they have this life as concrete fleshly creatures, embedded in this world. The "I" that stands before God and lives in God is the "I" engaged with food and wars, with other people's bodies and other people's voices. Nowhere is a man disengaged from the realm of immediate experience, that is, from his body. That is where God's act in Christ touches him anew each day for judgment and mercy. That is where God's word works anew each day to produce the fruit of repentence and charity in him. That is where he is called anew each day to the service of his neighbors' concrete needs. Members of the Christian community always exist as flesh, as perceptually engaged with the things around them. Their call to be Christians is a call for them to live exactly where they are, because exactly where they are is the place in which God shares his eternal life with them through Jesus Christ.

From this point of view, poetry's celebration of concrete experience is perfectly congenial with the Christian life. A Christian need have no fear that it might distract him from his "heavenly" destiny, because his road to that destiny takes him into the very realm that poetry presents. Poetry, of course, does not provide a man with a substitute for his own continuing movement into the actual. He does not learn of God's grace or wrestle obediently with the needs of his neighbor by reading verse. Yet such reading is a natural part of his constant openness to the immediate world, his constant readiness for the judgments and promises and needs that meet him there. He can enjoy poetry's power to catch the flash and sting of concrete experience. He can let it reveal to him a richer reality than he usually notices during his daily preoccupations. He can freely submit to the spell of its words, without having to inquire into its "world-view" or make it a tool for cultural diagnosis.

It is not enough, however, simply to say that poetry can be legitimately enjoyed within the Christian community. In terms of one special problem, it provides a crucial service. For Christians are constantly tempted to ignore their own fleshliness. Their flesh is the realm of their weakness, of their need, and above all, of their death. It reminds them of their dependence on physical things such as food and shelter. It is the ever present witness of their mortality, that they do not possess life in themselves but must be constantly nourished by reality, that even under the grace of God they remain earthen vessels subject to death, since the power of life belongs to God and not to them.

(II Cor. 4:7.) Flesh, one might say, is the arena of man's humiliation.

The temptation toward spiritual pride, therefore, always involves the evasion or suppression of flesh. When so tempted, a person begins to dream of meeting God in terms of his strength, rather than in terms of his weakness. He begins to identify himself with the religious beliefs and spiritual values of his withdrawn mind, rather than with the concrete fleshly creature that he is, flowing in and with the world. He begins to locate his moral life, not in what he actually does toward and for his neighbors, but in the invisible intentions that are supposed to be inside his heart. He hopes to be blessed because of the strength of his inner convictions, and not because of the needs of his engaged vitality. He does not want to be an earthen vessel, but a spiritual atmosphere.

Yet in all this he reverses his true situation. His flesh as the realm of his weakness and mortality does not alienate him from God, but draws him to God. Christian faith is not an activity of the withdrawn mind, concerned in arranging itself in a "correct" posture and possessing the "right" set of beliefs. Faith is confidence in God as the Lord of the here and now, as the One who became our flesh, who sustains our flesh, and who graces our flesh, so that He may finally glorify us in the flesh. Faith therefore gives men the freedom to be what they are, concrete mortal creatures openly engaged with the world, assured that in that condition God gives his life to them and in that condition they are called to give their lives to each other. Christian charity is not the activity of the withdrawn will, which retreats from a situation in order to prop itself up in a "Christian attitude," and then returns to see what good deeds it can do. Christian charity, including the work of prayer, moves in response to the immediate impact of fleshly experience and the immediate perception of fleshly needs. "Remember those who are in prison, as though in prison with them, and those who are ill-treated, since you also are in the body." (Heb. 13:3.) "If anyone gives so much as a cup of cold water to one of these little ones, because he is a disciple of mine, I say to you, he shall have his reward." (Matt. 10:42.)

It is in terms of the temptation to spiritual pride that poetry performs a vital service in the Christian community. It reminds a man where he and his neighbors are actually living their existence each day. It reveals some of the weight and depth of immediate experience and by comparison exposes the unreality of so many human preoccupations. Most important of all, it keeps the Christian community aware of the kind of speech which for each generation lies closest to their concrete life.

For spiritual pride not only perverts the attitudes of Christian people. It also affects their language. The more a man removes his Christian life from the sphere of his immediate experiences, the more difficult it will be for him to talk about it in everyday speech. His spiritual pride will force him to create an artificial technical language for Christian truth, and to put all vernacular speech under a cloud of suspicion. He puts his life in Christ far away from the world of ordinary conversation. It can be properly articulated only by an unnatural discourse.

A technical language certainly has its place in the Christian community. It serves to guide Christians as they think and speak of God in the ordinary idiom of their day. Scripture, creeds, and theological studies must always perform this function. But whenever such technical language becomes an end in itself and is taken as the only true language in the church, whenever sermons and prayers are content to repeat theologically precise abstractions, then Christians are saying that their true life with God separates them from the present concrete world, and from the everyday speech that belongs to that world. They are evading their enfleshed condition. By calling attention to the freshness and scope of daily speech, poetry calls the Christian community away from a one-sided preoccupation with its own technical language.

One thing must be emphasized, however. Both in this service and in the recovery of immediate experience, the Christian community is not primarily interested in poetry by Christian believers about their Christian experiences. If verse is written by such persons, as occasionally it is, all well and good. But in terms of the constant tendency of Christians to evade rather than to celebrate their existence as flesh, what is needed is good poetry, fresh and vigorous poetry—whoever the author and whatever his personal religion. What the Christian seeks is the actuality of immediate experience, and for that he may find the works of an unbelieving pagan far more effective than anything written by his fellow Christians. He has a legitimate interest in *poetry as such*, in the power of its rhythms and in the freshness of its metaphors. He does not have to concern himself with the private religion of its author, or the topical relevance of its subject matter. Even six lines on the waning moon can recall him to his perceptual life in the flesh.

VI.

The three chapters that follow are really case studies of the way in which poems, as poems, may have a valuable impact upon the Christian community.

Each study is concerned with one kind of poetic language, and with the aspect of immediate experience that it brings into focus. Then the question is raised whether that poetry points up any particular kinds of evasion that now trouble the Christian community.

NOTES FOR CHAPTER ONE

1. T. E. Hulme, *Speculations* (New York: Harcourt, Brace & Co., 1924), p. 134.
2. Wallace Stevens, *Opus Posthumous*, ed. Samuel French Morse (New York: Alfred A. Knopf, Inc., 1957), p. 226.
3. *Ibid.*, p. 236.
4. Saint Augustine *Confessions* X.vi.8.

Chapter Two

City Speech: T. S. Eliot

I SHALL BEGIN WITH T. S. Eliot (born 1888).[1] Since 1927 his literary work has been emphatically Christian in its orientation. Not since Coleridge has a man of such theological sophistication wielded so much influence in poetry. For those who are interested in the literary expression of Christian doctrine, or in the aesthetics of a Christian artist, or in a Christian encounter with the modern world, the later work of Eliot is fundamental. My interest, however, is not in the Christianity of poets, but in their poetic language, understanding this as a recovery of concrete experience. From this point of view, Eliot's earlier work is more interesting, and especially his famous poem *The Waste Land* (1922).

Almost everything possible and impossible has been written about this poem. What has not always been emphasized, however, is the sound of its language to the listening ear. For more than any other single work, it helped to bring about a dramatic revolution in the *music* of English and American poetry. It ended the rule of one group of poetic sounds, and inaugurated the reign of another. And it did this by concerning itself with a wholly new domain of concrete experience. It broke the grip of the old poetry because its new style was alive with the freshness of a new aspect of immediacy.

We must now seek to understand how *The Waste Land* brought this new language into poetry, and how it made men aware of a new area of their experience. It is here, and not just in his later, more conspicuously religious verse, that Eliot serves the life of the Christian community.

I.

The prevailing style from which Eliot broke away is familiar to everyone. Here is an example taken at random, the opening stanza of Laurence Binyon's "Initiation" (1920).

> The wind has fallen asleep; the bough that tost
> Is quiet; the warm sun's gone; the wide light
> Sinks and is almost lost;
> Yet the April day glows on within my mind
> Happy as the white buds in the blue air,
> A thousand buds that shone on waves of wind.
> Now evening leads me wooingly apart.
> The young wood draws me down these shelving ways
> Deeper, as if it drew me to its heart.

The scene is nature, but the mood is one of dreamy ease. The jarring rawness of life has been set aside. Out of dusk and woods, the poetry has created a situation in which the human spirit can relax and let itself be entranced by the soft beauties around it.

In this peculiar complex of factors—the scene of natural beauty, the mellifluous language, and the mood of soothing relaxation—we have the type of poetry that prevailed in England and America before the First World War. To read poetry meant to enter a world without any frustrating hardness, a world perfectly in tune with the wish of the human heart, in short, a world where dreams of pleasure were not disturbed by obstructions from reality. Often the pleasurable loveliness of nature was expanded to include the pleasurable love between a man and a woman. Styles varied. Some writers, such as Binyon, preferred a heavy-handed rhetoric. Others, such as A. E. Housman, worked for a clean effect. In all this variety, however, the main features of beautiful nature, sweet language, and inner relaxation usually prevailed.

What propelled poetry in this direction was the enveloping oppressiveness of the modern industrial city. All this poetry came from city people, who, from their paved streets and closed rooms, looked at the seeming quietness of nature and imagined there an idyllic world of peace and contentment. We find this flight from the city already beginning to attract poetry early in the nineteenth century.

> Stranger, if thou hast learned a truth which needs
> No school of long experience, that the world
> Is full of guilt and misery, and hast seen
> Enough of all its sorrows, crimes, and cares,
> To tire thee of it, enter this wild wood
> And view the haunts of Nature. The calm shade
> Shall bring a kindred calm, and the sweet breeze
> That makes the green leaves dance, shall waft a balm
> To thy sick heart. Thou wilt find nothing here
> Of all that pained thee in the haunts of men,
> And made thee loathe thy life.

William Cullen Bryant published this poem, entitled "Inscription for the Entrance to a Wood," in 1821, but the same could be heard everywhere in 1901. People then were reading Yeats's "The Lake Isle of Innisfree," or Richard Hovey's "The Sea Gypsy," or John Masefield's "Sea Fever," or Arthur Symons' "In the Wood of Finvara":

> I have grown tired of sorrow and human tears;
> Life is a dream in the night, a fear among fears,
> A naked runner lost in a storm of spears.
>
> .   .   .   .
>
> I would wash the dust of the world in a soft green
>   flood;
> Here between sea and sea, in the fairy wood,
> I have found a delicate, wave-green solitude.
>
> Here in the fairy wood, between sea and sea,
> I have heard the song of a fairy bird in a tree,

> And the peace that is not in the world has flown
> to me.

Poetry was able to give people in the city a sense of the immediate feel of hushed woods and gentle breezes. It could redeem them, for a moment, from the jarring suffocation of their urban existence. It could transport them to a world free from the congestion of crowds or the boredom of work, without the materialistic rationalism of science or the utilitarian rationalism of business. "I would be a bird," Robert Bridges wrote, and in that vein most of the poets were soaring up or sailing off or dreaming away to some sylvan glen.

We can describe the function of all this poetry in the most general terms by calling it a poetry of *exaltation*. Poems existed in order to exalt life beyond its daily tawdriness, and poets usually chose their subject matter and fashioned their diction on that basis. Anything ordinary, mean, or base was none of their business. Their duty was to show forth the inspiring character of things, and by means of their poetic language to help people to appreciate what was above the ordinary. This poetry naturally preferred an elevated style. If someone such as Kipling used crude language in his verse, and had his soldiers saying "extry rations" and "cookroom slops," this was only to set off by contrast the elevated moral grandeur that glowed inside their hearts.

It is interesting to note that even the city itself was made a subject for poetry, whenever its ugliness was concealed by a lovely coating from nature. For Wordsworth, who looked at it from a distance, it sparkled in the early sunlight, and "now doth like a garment wear/The beauty of the morning" (1802). William Morris saw it "small and white and clean" as it was in Chaucer's time (1868). Robert Bridges portrayed it covered with dazzling snow (1880), and W. E. Henley, in "London Voluntaries," bathed in golden sunlight (1893).

> For earth and sky and air
> Are golden everywhere,
> And golden with a gold so suave and fine

The looking on it lifts the heart like wine.
Trafalgar Square
(The fountains volleying golden glaze)
Shines like an angel-market. High aloft
Over his couchant Lions, in a haze
Shimmering and bland and soft,
A dust of chrysoprase,
Our Sailor takes the golden gaze
Of the saluting sun, and flames superb,
As once he flamed it on his ocean round.

This poetry of exaltation had nothing to say about the ordinary city. Its obligation was to record the moments of rare beauty, when things could "lift the heart like wine."

No one can deny the power of the experiences that sustained this poetry. What was disastrous was the narrow preoccupation with just this one topic for so many decades. Instead of giving itself to the recovery of fresh immediacy, poetry began to mark out certain kinds of language and certain kinds of topics as *its* province, to be defined once and for all as "poetic." Other language enterprises, such as science or politics, were forbidden to touch these. Thus, instead of serving the human consciousness, poetry began to serve itself, and to perpetuate its control over the areas that it had marked out as its own.

The place where we see this perversion most clearly is in the poetic diction that flourished during this period. For when the poets became concerned about preserving and perpetuating a particular kind of identity for themselves, when they tried to put their own claim on one particular kind of language, then they stopped listening to the ever changing pattern of daily speech, where the impact of immediacy first comes to crude expression. They withdrew poetry into a technically artificial language of its own, and so unwittingly cut it off from its living root. Listen to these lines from "A Passer-by" by Robert Bridges.

Whither, O splendid ship, thy white sails crowding,
Leaning across the bosom of the urgent West,

That fearest nor sea rising nor sky clouding,
Whither away, fair rover, and what thy quest?

This style is certainly "poetic," in the sense that it perpetuates a way of writing poetry which had become standardized, which everyone agreed to honor as "poetic," and which therefore gave the poet a distinctive empire of his own. But in the latter part of the nineteenth century, such language as this had lost all touch with the concrete life of men. There was no justification for its metaphors and rhythms. Its verbal artificialities did not grow from a living engagement with the real. They were simply sustained by the poet's arbitrary will to be "poetic."

It would be to misunderstand the situation completely to imagine that the poets of this period passively acquiesced in this dominant mode. The task of saying something fresh—that is, of saying something less lovely, less mellifluously relaxing than the nature poetry of the day—was everybody's problem. Thomas Hardy tried for roughness; A. E. Housman, for irony; Edwin Arlington Robinson, for character puzzles; Arthur Symons, for decadence; and Alfred Noyes, for folk vigor. All developed new styles. To us who look back, however, the astonishing thing is that during this whole period no one carried poetic diction in the one direction that would obviously restore it to contemporary life. No one absorbed into verse *the daily speech and the daily immediacy of the city.* While experiments abounded, none were radical enough. They only modified the tones and points of view. They did not reach down and throw away the fundamental music that lay at the heart of this prevailing diction. They did not turn their backs on the music of exaltation, in favor, say, of the music of ordinary speech. They did not take to the city streets. For this achievement poetry had to wait for T. S. Eliot's *The Waste Land.*

II.

Of course, Eliot did not develop his new poetic language all at once. The two volumes of his poetry that preceded *The Waste*

Land are very instructive in showing the stages by which his style evolved.

One might say that in his first volume, published in 1917, he succeeded in taking the details of city existence and making valid poetic images out of them. That is, he brought into English verse a domain of images that French poetry had been fashioning for half a century. At one level, this meant a change in locale. Instead of dealing with verdant fields and tossing boughs, Eliot's lines wove a texture of sensations from the city.

> Half-past one,
> The street-lamp sputtered,
> The street-lamp muttered,
> The street-lamp said, "Regard that woman
> Who hesitates toward you in the light of the door
> Which opens on her like a grin.
> You see the border of her dress
> Is torn and stained with sand,
> And you see the corner of her eye
> Twists like a crooked pin."

We are in the midst of vacant lots and muddy streets,

> Of restless nights in one-night cheap hotels
> And sawdust restaurants with oyster-shells.

And everywhere we are assaulted by smells—"the smells of steaks in passageways," the "female smells in shuttered rooms," the smells of "cigarettes in corridors/And cocktail smells in bars."

The mere accumulation of details from the city scene does not, of course, make poetic images. There must also be a realization of the feelings and the sense of the world that are associated with these details. They must be given a special intensity, such as Eliot himself notes in the work of Baudelaire.

> It is not merely in the use of imagery of common life, not merely in the use of imagery of the sordid life of a great metropolis, but in the elevation of such imagery to the first

intensity—presenting it as it is, and yet making it represent something much more than itself—that Baudelaire has created a mode of release and expression for other men.[2]

This intensity, this larger reference is what Eliot achieves in his first volume. In and through the sights and smells of the city, he articulates the sense of a world from which all interpersonal relationships have been eliminated. Here, for instance, is his portrayal of morning in "Preludes."

> The morning comes to consciousness
> Of faint stale smells of beer
> From the sawdust-trampled street
> With all its muddy feet that press
> To early coffee-stands.
> With the other masquerades
> That time resumes,
> One thinks of all the hands
> That are raising dingy shades
> In a thousand furnished rooms.

This passage is not simply a description of beer smells, coffee stands, and dingy shades. These are part of a larger pattern in which the consciousness never knows a human being. It only hears feet along the sidewalk and sees hands upon the blinds. It only encounters people as fragmentary things in an endless chaos of things. Persons are withdrawn from each other, remaining perpetual strangers. How can it be otherwise in this world of chance meetings and ever changing acquaintanceships? They can never give or reveal themselves, but only keep preparing their faces to meet other faces.

The title poem in this volume—"The Love Song of J. Alfred Prufrock"—is the monologue of a middle-aged man, trying to build up his courage to declare his love to some woman, and failing. While it is a fascinating character sketch, the focus is not on the character but on the total situation. There is an ever present sense of the city, so that Prufrock's feeling of helplessness does not appear as a private peculiarity of his own, but

as the inevitable consequence of the world that envelops him
—the endless, half-deserted streets, the fog, the empty chatter
of social gatherings, the eyes of other people that are always
fixing him, assessing him, pinning him wriggling on the wall. In
a city of a million strangers, how can anyone take his own life
seriously, much less, in the name of love, expect some other person to do so? In Prufrock's middle-aged helplessness, Eliot has
created an image of the whole tenor of human existence in the
city, for young and old alike.

In these early poems, we can see the level at which Eliot begins to reorient poetry. Verse, he shows, does not have to limit
itself to presenting a pleasure world where human yearnings
are fulfilled. It can also do just the opposite, and actualize a
realm of perpetual frustration. Because of its power to actualize
immediate experience, it has as much to do with suffering as with
exaltation.

The authority of these early poems by Eliot lay in their
powerful recovery of immediate experience. It was not that he believed in original sin, or had some private quirk in his own personality that made it hard for him to appreciate human beings.
It was simply that he brought into focus a quality that belonged
to the immediate impact of the city. Anyone who walks along
a city street is besieged by such a confusing flood of objects that
his mind never has a chance to identify the personal factor. At
the level of his immediate experience, human beings are ob-
scured behind the blur of honking horns, blinking lights, and
shoving bodies. For the person who lives alone in a succession of
boarding houses and works in a succession of standardized jobs,
there may be no encounter with the personal reality of other
people from one year to the next, and therefore no understanding of a personal name. The identifying labels for the breakfast
foods that stand in the pantry, the automobiles that pass on the
street, and the individuals that live across the hall are all on the
same level.

> Half-past two,
> The street-lamp said,

"Remark the cat which flattens itself in the gutter,
Slips out its tongue
And devours a morsel of rancid butter."
So the hand of the child, automatic,
Slipped out and pocketed a toy that was running
          along the quay.
I could see nothing behind that child's eye.
I have seen eyes in the street
Trying to peer through lighted shutters,
And a crab one afternoon in a pool,
An old crab with barnacles on his back,
Gripped the end of a stick which I held him.

In spite of their refreshing novelty, these first poems have a
serious weakness. It lies in their verbal music. Their images and
the suffering that they express certainly belong to the city, but
again and again they echo the melodious richness of the prevailing style, and call to mind a world far away from urban congestion. There is "a soft October night." There are peaceful after-
noons and evenings. There are soft voices "dying with a dying
fall." One poem paints a romantic moment from figures on a
vase. "Prufrock" closes with a vision of mermaids—a vision which
is stated to be unreal, but which rings with such a striking and
evocative music that it makes the ear forget the city. It is as if
Eliot still felt the need to reinforce his verse with a little bit of
exaltation.

This limitation in the early poems reflects a problem, and not
just a failure. The city, it must be remembered, is not simply a
place of sights and smells and feelings, but also of sounds. Noises
there tend to have certain distinguishing qualities—a competi-
tive harshness, a dissonance, a pounding rhythm. Wherever
men live, they unconsciously absorb the prevailing sound qualities of their immediate surroundings into their own speech,
especially at the level of rhythm. This is as true in the city as elsewhere. A man who converses on a sidewalk must compete with
all sorts of other urban noises, and therefore he shows a prefer-
ence for vocal sounds that can be made loud easily. City speech
becomes standardized and uniform, so that others can grasp it

quickly. In the welter of ever flowing objects and ever changing faces, this language must also be able, within brief compasses of time, to adapt to the most unbelievable variety of situations, without incoherent adjustments. That is, it must be able to move swiftly and yet hold itself at the level of matter-of-fact flatness, where it can easily pick up and drop whatever happens to claim attention. A businessman at lunch might be heard saying:

> I have to go now, Jim; I'll pay the bill to the waitress. Well, hello, Jerry. It's been a long time since we've met in town. How's Janet? . . . You were divorced last year? I didn't know that. I'm sorry. Oh, Jim, have you got change for the tip? Good-by, Jerry. . . . Ready, Jim, I want to pick up a paper. I'm worried about the weather for a party we're having tomorrow night. Look at these headlines! War in Angola again. Oops—pardon me, fellow . . . What's that? . . . No, there is a Perkins Street about four blocks from here, but I've never heard of Perdue Street . . . [Etc., etc., etc.]

Speech in the city absorbs the sounds and jumbled chaos of its environment.

The problem that becomes clear in Eliot's first poems is that this disjointed, wholly standardized, and uniformly flat speech of city life does not seem to have enough music in it to merit the rhythmic capacity of poetry. It is essentially anti-poetic. It may be able to describe the sordid urban sights and may be able to voice a man's anguished feeling of isolation. But when it begins to fill stanza after stanza of poetry, it quickly becomes repetitive and dull. Its inherent flatness takes away the possibility of rhythmic variety, of a rise and fall in intensity. This is what Eliot's ear must have sensed in these poems of 1917. To do justice to their own poetic nature, they had to have "a soft October night" and singing mermaids "riding seaward on the waves." Otherwise, they seemed to be in danger of collapsing into prose. From the very beginning, then, Eliot found himself confronting what seemed to be an impasse. If poetry was to sink itself into the language, as well as into the sensations and feelings, of the city, how could it remain poetically interesting?

Eliot's next volume of verse appeared in 1920, and achieved a much more intense awareness of the agony of city life. The world that wears against the mind is no longer marked simply by a lack of humanity. It is a world riddled through and through with death, and devoid of *every* kind of vitality. We stand in a universe without color, without fresh air, without health, without purpose, and without glory. Signs are taken for wonders. Church sacraments, works of art, and sexual intercourse have all become ends in themselves, rather than the media for a richness from beyond them. As such they give no nourishment to human existence. They serve only as distractions. Encounter with other people is no longer found shocking, because of their lack of humanity, because we are able to "see nothing behind their eyes." What now dominates Eliot's lines is the experience of their animal brutality. Human history has lost all moral significance, all capacity for the enormities of good and evil. It is simply the record of crude human animals, moved by vanity, manipulated by circumstance, and led to no particular end but death.

> Neither fear nor courage saves us. Unnatural vices
> Are fathered by our heroism. Virtues
> Are forced upon us by our impudent crimes.
> These tears are shaken from the wrath-bearing tree.

One might say that in these poems of 1920 the city has ceased to be an identifiable place in the external world, and has become the glasses—or microcosm—through which the whole universe is seen. The dominant tone is now one of revulsion.

When we look at how Eliot has realized this world poetically, we find a very unusual device. Again and again he sets present-day scenes side by side with similar scenes from the past, letting the ugliness of the one be set off by the grandeur of the other. For instance, he presents two modern American tourists in Venice, one of whom hires a prostitute while the other looks at

paintings. Between descriptions of them, however, Eliot inserts
two stanzas that echo lines from Shakespeare's *Antony and
Cleopatra*. These evoke a sense of the bygone glory that now
has vanished from Venice and from love.

> Burbank crossed a little bridge
>   Descending at a small hotel;
> Princess Volupine arrived,
>   They were together, and he fell.
>
> Defunctive music under sea
>   Passed seaward with the passing bell
> Slowly: the God Hercules
>   Had left him, that had loved him well.
>
> The horses, under the axletree
>   Beat up the dawn from Istria
> With even feet. Her shuttered barge
>   Burned on the water all the day.
>
> But this or such was Bleistein's way:
>   A saggy bending of the knees
> And elbows, with the palms turned out,
>   Chicago Semite Viennese.
>
> A lustreless protrusive eye
>   Stares from the protozoic slime
> At a perspective of Canaletto.

The revulsive impact of Bleistein is complicated and enlarged by
the realization of the glories that he has replaced.

Another poem describes a touring honeymoon couple in bed
at a hotel in Ravenna, Italy, sweating in the summer heat and
scratching the bug bites over their flabby legs, while nearby the
great crumbling basilica of St. Apollinaris still holds its grandeur.
Again, the murder of the Greek king Agamemnon is contrasted
with a plot by two girls in a bar to steal from one of the cus-
tomers. In still another poem, Eliot compares the dreadful deser-
tion of Ariadne by the Greek hero Theseus with a mean incident
in a modern boarding house. A woman tenant there is shrieking

with epileptic convulsions, while an utterly indifferent man
listens and continues his shaving.

> Sweeney addressed full length to shave
> Broadbottomed, pink from nape to base,
> Knows the female temperament
> And wipes the suds around his face.

> (The lengthened shadow of a man
> Is history, said Emerson
> Who had not seen the silhouette
> Of Sweeney straddled in the sun.)

> Tests the razor on his leg
> Waiting until the shriek subsides.
> The epileptic on the bed
> Curves backward, clutching at her sides.

In these poems there is no lack of poetic intensity, no danger
of prosaic dullness. The images of grandeur and of revulsion
stand in the sharpest juxtaposition, and both are carried to the
highest pitch. Eliot, however, has paid a price for this intensity.
He had had to move away from the kind of language that is
actually heard in the city. This verse has none of the snatches
of conversation or the rhythms of the speaking voice that were
used so effectively in the first volume. Such an explosive savagery
and disgust lie on the surface of the lines that the language has
to be put in a rigidly artificial form, to keep the emotion under
some control. In this way, the severely simple four-line stanzas
and the constant discipline of rhyming provide a kind of counter-
pressure. The revulsion is thus kept under restraint. The past
grandeur and present degradation of man can be expressed with
a startling directness, without the language being shaken into
chaos.

This conspicuous presence of form means that as we read, we
are aware that this is the work of the individual poet. The sense
of grandeur in the past and the feeling of revulsion for the present are not presented as ingredients in the common language and
common consciousness, which the poet has simply brought to

the surface. These are the poet's own feelings, which he has to express in and through a language pattern of his own devising. That is, as far as the ear can tell, these emotions exist primarily in the poet's consciousness.

What was true of the first poems of 1917, therefore, still remained true in 1920. Eliot continued to find that as a poet he could not realize the immediate impact of the city by using the living speech of city people. While he eliminated dreams and romantic fancies, he still needed an artificially severe form to sustain his poetic music. To put this another way, Eliot had not yet found the suffering which informs man's city life in the actual language of the city. He had to articulate it by means of verbal creations of his own.

The Waste Land, which appeared two years later in 1922, is primarily significant as the climax of Eliot's urbanization of poetry. Here he carries his revolution of poetic diction into the whole texture of his verse. What happens is, first, that the kind of sickening vision which leaps at the reader immediately from every line of the 1920 poems comes into focus only very slowly and gradually, by a progression of carefully arranged stages in the verse; and secondly, that this focus is achieved entirely with the kind of verbal music that is actually heard every day on the city streets. In other words, *The Waste Land* does not depend on dreamy visions, or artificial stanzas, or shocking contrasts with the past to sustain its poetic music. In its main thread, it stays immersed within the language of the city, and yet is able, through that medium, to bring the agony of urban existence into full focus.

III.

Most commentators have not been able to enjoy *The Waste Land* in terms of its poetry. They have been constantly distracted by the fact that the whole poem is larded with innumerable phrases taken from earlier works of literature. While no effort is made within the poem to call attention to these—say, by

quotation marks or parenthetical references—Eliot has provided
a number of pages of notes at the end of the work, where he
indicates the sources that he has used.

For instance, after giving us brief snatches of various conver-
sations from the city scene, Part I closes with a look at the city
en bloc.

> Unreal City,
> Under the brown fog of a winter dawn,
> A crowd flowed over London Bridge, so many,
> I had not thought death had undone so many.
> Sighs, short and infrequent, were exhaled,
> And each man fixed his eyes before his feet.
> Flowed up the hill and down King William Street,
> To where Saint Mary Woolnoth kept the hours
> With a dead sound on the final stroke of nine.

It is a normal London scene at the beginning of the day, as
office workers pour toward their various buildings. The lines
emphasize the deathlike quality of these people, with their perpetually tired sighs and their dumb mechanical plodding. The
last stroke of nine, when office work officially begins, rings out
with a dead sound. Although the lines form a unified and coherent whole, they are certainly not very intense. We have only
to remember the violent revulsion in the poems of 1920 to realize
the low level of intensity that characterizes this verse. Compared
to what Eliot could do with flabby faces and dead eyes, the sense
of lifelessness here is kept subdued.

If we consult the notes, we find all sorts of surprises. For instance, the phrase "Unreal City" is apparently an echo from a
poem by Baudelaire, where the modern metropolis is presented
as a kind of nightmare world in which dreams and realities are
indistinguishable. Again, the words about death having "undone
so many" and about the "sighs" short and infrequent are actually
taken from the early part of Dante's *Inferno*, where Dante is
describing the fate of souls who are neither destined for eternal
joy nor damned for deliberate evil. Research by professors has
also discovered that the eerie dead sound from the church bell

is reminiscent of the perilous chapel in the grail legends of the Middle Ages. These legends, Eliot tells us in an opening note, provide much material for the poem.

Now it is immediately evident that, in presenting a human world of deathly unreality to the reader's listening ear, Eliot's own words make a relatively faint impact compared to what we find in Baudelaire or Dante or, in a different sense, in the grail legends. Precisely at this point the now conventional approach to *The Waste Land* has taken a hold. Since Eliot's own language is never poetically intense, and is sometimes downright obscure, and since he himself has given us references to works in which the same scene is powerfully presented, he must want us to think of these other works when we read his lines. In the passage just quoted, then, we are to look at London as Eliot presents it in his lines. At the same time, however, we are to have the surprise of seeing that this modern London is also Baudelaire's nightmare city, and further still that it is a world without beatitude or damnation, such as Dante found at the opening of hell.

Thus arises the dedicated effort by scholars to trace out all the hidden quotations that fill *The Waste Land*, to read and absorb the works from which they come, and then to read the poem in terms of the perspectives that these other works present. In other words, the poem does not itself actualize the sense of the city that it wants to give. Instead, by means of the hidden quotations, it directs the reader to those other books, and counts on his memory of them to make its points. F. O. Matthiessen explains this technique, in reference to the passage about the "Unreal City." In these references to Baudelaire and Dante, he says, "Eliot is not making mere literary allusions. He is not imitating these poets; nor has he mistaken literature for life. Each of these references brings with it the weight of its special context, its authentic accent of reality, and thus enables Eliot to condense into a single passage a concentrated expression of tragic horror." [3] According to this view of the poem, then, each fragment is given in order to remind the reader of its perspective. When these perspectives are seen in juxtaposition, and are compared with the contemporary scene that Eliot sketches in his own words, then all kinds of illuminating resonances are produced in the reader's mind. Above all, he sees that the poem is a massive and terrifying judgment on the modern world. By comparison with the beliefs and meanings found in the books of other ages, he realizes how empty is the language of his own world.

A person's enjoyment of *The Waste Land* therefore depends on how readily he can respond to these hidden references, and on how quickly and effortlessly his mind can be triggered by them to remember the books from which they come. He must master the notes and absorb an intellectual background *before* he can feel the impact of the poetry. According to this view, a reader oblivious to the references to Baudelaire and Dante cannot possibly find in Eliot's own words "a concentrated expression of tragic horror."

In the discussion that follows, I will not pursue this customary allusionist method. For it actually implies that *The Waste Land* is not successful as a poem, is not successful insofar as it works immediately upon the listening ear with its imagery and music. In fact, this is the point made by almost all of those who concentrate on the notes. The knowledge of Baudelaire and Dante is necessary, they acknowledge, because there is *not enough poetic intensity in the verbal impact of Eliot's own lines*. We must supplement what we hear from his poem with a recollection of what was said in the other books, because that is the way to convert his subdued passages, such as the one about the "Unreal City," into "a concentrated expression of tragic horror." It must be recognized, however, that if we have to enjoy the work in this way, we have ceased to read it as a poem. We are not submitting to its auditory spell, but are meditating under its guidance on a variety of other works. We have achieved an experience of horror, not poetically from what the ear hears, but intellectually by a relatively abstract effort of literary recollection.

In rejecting the allusionist method, then, I am really rejecting the judgment that *The Waste Land* is poetically inadequate. As my operating principle I shall take the view that the notes are irrelevant, that the poem has an overpowering clarity and meaning for the listening ear, and that its achievement at this level is what explains its continuing popularity and justifies its enormous influence. The notes may indicate what is not realized in this work and what must be found elsewhere—the experience that the modern city is a nightmare world, for instance, or the realization that men live at too low a level even to be included in hell. The ear, however, finds the meaning of the poem, not in these other books, but in the lines that it hears, "by listening to what is being communicated instead of looking for something that isn't." [4] The poem must stand in terms of its *own* verbal actuality. The researched memory of other books has no place. If references play a part, it is only because here and there the ear has been jostled into remembering a play by Shakespeare or a Greek myth.

That *The Waste Land* is indeed a poem for the listening ear is confirmed by the power it has when it is heard read aloud. That is the real test for the irrelevance of the notes. One can only report what is said not only by experienced readers but by uninstructed young people as well, that when they sit down and listen to one of the recordings of the poem, they find its impact unforgettable. In this situation they are not conscious of hidden allusions. They are not looking for "clues," or doing research, or investigating esoteric ancient myths with the help of anthropological monographs by Jessie Weston. The ear submits and is fulfilled. Apparently the poem does live in its verbal impact, apart from any hidden apparatus. Apparently the obscurity that has driven so many commentators to the notes is somehow at the auditory level gathered into a satisfying whole.

Finally, we must observe that the notes themselves are not at all as helpful as the allusionist approach would have us believe. For instance, what are we to do with the information that the dead sound in the bell of St. Mary Woolnoth's is an actual fact, which Eliot has "often noticed"? Or with the fact that Eliot does not know the origin of the ballad about the moon shining bright on Mrs. Porter, though "it was reported to me from Sydney, Australia"? Does Sydney, Australia, perhaps figure in some vegetative myth? Of what significance is the fact that the hermit-thrush mentioned in Part V is actually *Turdus aonalsch-kae pallasii;* that it is most at home in secluded woodlands according to one ornithologist (author and title duly given); and, *mirabile dictu,* that it has actually been heard by Eliot himself in—hold your hat on this one—Quebec County? This scrupulous and utterly pointless report on sources sounds to my ear like a very funny caricature of the whole enterprise of footnotes. As if footnotes could make any statement true. Certainly Eliot's own explanation of why he added so many notes should prevent us from taking them seriously.

When it came to print *The Waste Land* as a little book . . . it was discovered that the poem was inconveniently short, so I set to work to expand the notes, in order to provide a few more pages of printed matter. . . . They became the remarkable exposition of bogus scholarship that is still on view today. I have sometimes thought of getting rid of these notes, but . . . they have had almost greater popularity than the poem itself. . . . I regret having sent so many enquirers off on a wild goose chase after Tarot cards and the Holy Grail.[5]

IV.

The Waste Land is divided into five parts, and Eliot entitles the first "The Burial of the Dead." It is a remarkable realization of what can only be called the non-poetry of city speech. Here is the opening stanza.

> April is the cruellest month, breeding
> Lilacs out of the dead land, mixing
> Memory and desire, stirring
> Dull roots with spring rain.
> Winter kept us warm, covering
> Earth in forgetful snow, feeding
> A little life with dried tubers.
> Summer surprised us, coming over the
>   Starnbergersee

> With a shower of rain; we stopped in the colonnade,
> And went on in sunlight, into the Hofgarten,
> And drank coffee, and talked for an hour.
> Bin gar keine Russin, stamm' aus Litauen, echt
>   deutsch.
> And when we were children, staying at the
>   archduke's,
> My cousin's, he took me out on a sled,
> And I was frightened. He said, Marie,
> Marie, hold on tight. And down we went.
> In the mountains, there you feel free.
> I read, much of the night, and go south in the
>   winter.

At the most obvious level, where the mind tries to get some coherent grasp of who is speaking and what is being said, these lines are frustrating. Where is the Starnbergersee and the Hofgarten? What does the line in German say? The unexpected shifts in tone and subject matter suggest that these are snatches of conversation from several voices, but one cannot be sure. There is a confused jumble with no clear thread. Even the fact that the stanza describes the impact of three successive seasons of the year, and thus passes, as it were, through a full cycle of time, from winter through spring and summer and back to winter again, is carefully kept in the background. This organizing pattern is not allowed to break out upon the surface and alleviate the reader's sense of chaotic disorder.

Even more irritating than this surface confusion is the repeated collapse of poetic music. Every time the verse begins to gather a little rhythmic momentum and pulsate with the touch of some fresh experience, it is turned aside into flat prose. The surprising impact of summer gives a rising sweep to the lines, but this vitality is not continued. The rhythm slowly falls back into the monotony of routine existence, where we "drank coffee and talked for an hour," and where the conversation was, to the English ear, an empty blur of unintelligible German. The sense of exhilaration comes through much more strongly in the memory of sledding. "Marie,/Marie, hold on tight. And down we went." But here the rhythm collapses abruptly. A jaded adult voice speaks from a world without excitement, where reading has taken the place of life, and where severe weather is avoided by trips to the south.

This repeated collapse of the poetry communicates to the reader's ear that attitude which was stated in the opening lines. "April is the cruellest month." The impact of fresh life is to be avoided. This language and the consciousness that it reveals prefer a low level of existence. These speakers steer away from any vitality that threatens to approach them, maintaining themselves in sterile habits, "feeding/A little life with dried tubers." In this world it is only the child who enjoys the thrill of clinging to the sled and surrendering herself to the plunging slope and the pull of gravity. It is only the child who will endure the fear for the sake of the excitement. The adult is more prudent. He knows the danger. He lives in small doses, reading at night and going south in the winter.

In the next stanza things begin to pick up. There is a development, though not in terms of poetic intensity. The surface continues to be perplexing, with unexpected shifts and lines in a foreign language. What happens is that the avoidance of life, which seemed like a mere evasion in the first stanza, now appears to be motivated by a positive dread.

A voice begins to speak in the solemn style of Old Testament prophecy. It issues a judgment against this picayune existence of empty chatter and empty habit, proclaiming it to be a desolate, sun-baked wasteland, and calling men to come in under the shadow of a red rock. But to the surprise of our ears the voice offers no relief, no consolation. If you come into this shadow, it says, I will show you something more than an empty wasteland, something more than the dancing of your own shadow. "I will show you fear in a handful of dust." Instead of building up to some great disclosure of God, after the fashion of the Old Testament, or to a vision of redeemed life, the lines twist into a promise only of terror. The rising momentum of the rhythm is suddenly chilled.

In another abrupt transition, there immediately follow some

lines from a song in German, and then a voice speaks of an
ecstatic experience of romantic love.

> "You gave me hyacinths first a year ago;
> "They called me the hyacinth girl."
> —Yet when we came back, late, from the
>   Hyacinth garden,
> Your arms full, and your hair wet, I could not
> Speak, and my eyes failed, I was neither
> Living nor dead, and I knew nothing,
> Looking into the heart of light, the silence.
> *Oed' und leer das Meer.*

Here again the music of the lines deliberately disappoints us.
It sounds at first as though the verse were building up to a
beatific rapture, so familiar in love lyrics. But the words play a
trick on us, without our quite realizing it. They blur into vacuity
just at the critical moment. Instead of climaxing in a soaring cry
of exaltation, they give an uncanny impression of stunned paralysis. I could not speak, I could not see. There was nothing before
my mind and nothing upon my ear. Instead of an experience of
fulfillment, the reader is left with an obscure feeling of dread.
And this is continued for him into the last line. *"Oed' und leer
das Meer."* Presuming that his native language is English, these
German words give his ear no new content and no clearer picture of the situation. Their mournful sound simply underscores
the absence of expected joy, and reinforces his sense of dismay.

In this second stanza there has been no increase in "poetic"
beauty. Eliot continues his opening technique of starting a lyrical
momentum in the lines, and then destroying it. But there has
been a development in the atmosphere. Now the lyric intensity
is repeatedly stifled by fear, and not just by evasion. Thus a state
of mind begins to emerge from the lines, in which men fly from
the impact of life whenever it comes close to them. In quick
succession we have heard the verse turning away from the exhilarating impact of spring and summer and winter, and then away
from a prophetic call to divine judgment, and finally away from
the rapture of love. We are not shown the reasons for this nega-

tive response. It is just that the life-giving powers that can exalt men impose themselves upon the reading imagination in an unattractive way. They appear as a plunging sled ride, or an ominous shadow, or a paralyzing ecstasy.

All the rest of the opening part of the poem maintains this uneasy mood. There are the strange signs on the fortune teller's cards—a drowned Phoenician sailor, a one-eyed merchant, a hanged man—all unintelligible to the listening ear but all touched with foreboding. There is the "Unreal City" where men walk as if in a trance, and where the church bell gives off an eerie dead sound on the final stroke of nine. There is finally the closing encounter, where a man passing on the street is suddenly addressed and asked whether the corpse that he planted in his garden last year has begun to sprout and blossom yet. Here the feeling of unfocused dread rises into the grotesque.

Now why this dread? This is not what the poetry prevailing before Eliot had taught its readers to expect. On the contrary, they firmly believed that people liked spring and excitement, that they wanted to talk with each other intimately, that they craved to hear the Word of God and to enjoy romantic love. Verse was written on the assumption that, if real life didn't give men these satisfactions, then poetry could. Poetry had the task of fulfilling a man's simple urge for exaltation. How, then, can Eliot make these experiences a source of dread?

Though no reasons are given clearly in this first part of *The Waste Land*, there is still a kind of emotional logic about this fear. It is suggested by the adult voice that follows the excitement of the sled, and by the strange vacuity in the moment of love. Perhaps these intense experiences destroy man instead of exalting him. If a person abandons himself to some alien power—to spring, to divine judgment, to love—if he lets it possess him, lets it carry him wherever it will, can he be sure that it will fill him with life? Instead, might it not shake him and break him to pieces, with its violence? Look how germination shatters the seed, or the birth of a child may tear apart the mother. If we think of an opera such as Wagner's *Tristan und Isolde*, look how erotic love can destroy human beings. Will the touch of some new kind of life revive a man or stun him? Will it exalt him, or will it only whirl him to his doom with its unmanageable dynamism? If anyone thinks of submitting to some life-giving power, and stepping beyond the ordinary world of sterile habit and empty routine, he immediately confronts the possibility that this new "life" may consume him with fires that he cannot contain. Exaltation always shakes and destroys the ordinary forms of a person's life, and the thought of it therefore always arouses dread, as well as desire. "I dreaded the first robin so," Emily Dickinson wrote, for even the power of spring touches us with an alien vitality.

> I dared not meet the daffodils,
> For fear their yellow gown
> Would pierce me with a fashion
> So foreign to my own.

This ambivalent attitude toward exaltation has always been a familiar part of human experience. From primitive times it has been made explicit in the belief that anyone who wants to gain a new kind of life must first give up the life that now possesses him. The experience of self-transformation is therefore found only through a process of self-extinction. Every ritual of birth is also a ritual of death, an agonizing surrender to some life-giving power, with the real destruction of the old habits and the old self that this involves. The poetry that prevailed before Eliot completely ignored this ambivalence. Lovely nature, religious exaltation, and passionate love were all pursued without reservation, as if the human spirit had no qualms in being carried beyond its ordinary level of experience. This single-minded yearning for the infinite and the lovely gave this conventional poetry an inauthentic quality. It did not seem to be recovering the actual and agonizing impact of life-giving power, but to be creating a fictional world of uncomplicated pleasure.

The opening section of *The Waste Land* brings man's natural dread of life and fear of exaltation into the foreground. It does not portray this as a self-conscious theory or deliberate act of wisdom, however. The essence of dread lies precisely in the way in which it causes the mind to look *away* from that which it fears. These lines therefore indicate the situation to the listening ear without allowing it to come into clear focus. The lines keep disappointing us with their unfulfilled promises of lyric intensity, keep letting the sterile emptiness of city chatter and city confusion obscure all moments of poetic beauty. The ear is aware that in its lack of vitality this language exhibits a human wasteland. At the same time, this wasteland is never presented with unitary or cumulative coherence, by means of some unforgettable incident or richly developed image. For the reader, the sense of the wasteland keeps being lost amid the jumble of unmanageable fragments. At the same time, the ear is certainly made aware of the atmosphere of dread, of the feeling that all sources of fresh vitality are somehow dangerous. April is cruel, the shadow of the red rock seems ominous, the erotic ecstasy ends in empty paralysis. Yet here, too, the lines never bring this dread into clear focus. There is some lurking menace, but it is never clearly identified.

In their total effect, these passages give an overwhelming sense of *evasion*. Every promise of vitality and every emerging experience of dread are dissipated by some obstruction in the verse—a sudden shift of scene, a blurring of the imagery at the critical point, a line in some foreign language, which has no immediate content for English and American readers. And this blanket of evasiveness seems to be the working of an attitude of fear.

For the listening ear, this is a fascinating invitation into the poem. It is as if Eliot were conducting an experiment in tension, in which on the one hand he tries to keep close to the ordinary speech of the city, with its prosaic flatness and multilingual noise, and yet on the other hand, he tries to let the reader hear the strange undercurrent of fear that keeps this world in its sterile habits.

The poem, then, begins at the level of ordinary city talk, where all sense of horror and glory is so systematically avoided that no poetry is possible. The task that the poem sets for itself is to move beyond this initial stage of evasive unclarity, to give focus to these fundamental feelings—not in psychological terms, as if they were subjective entities that existed by themselves in someone's mind, but in poetic terms, as part of a man's living commerce with concrete immediacy. The poem is organized on the premise that people do not realize that they may be experiencing their daily routine as a wasteland which needs life, and may be experiencing the prospect of life as a dreadful convulsion which must be avoided. Only the most gradual clarifications, using all the resources of poetry, can carry the language beyond the fear-ridden evasiveness that pervades it, can draw other and more powerful kinds of verbal music out of daily speech.

The whole poem, then, will gradually bring into focus the significance of its title. It accepts its own responsibility on this point. It does not make the mistake of assuming either a) that a few images are enough to actualize the sterile impact that most city experience makes upon the consciousness, or b) that man's normal response to this sterility is a simple, single-minded quest for exaltation, such as we find in the poetry before Eliot. In the development of the poem, as each more vivid and immediately authentic realization of waste is attained, there not only develops an increasing desire to find some life-giving power, but also an increasing fear of the destructive capacities of such power. As a sense of the thirst for life intensifies, so also does the feeling of terror.

It is now possible to see how the notes and hidden references add an extra, but quite secondary, dimension to the poem for anyone who wants to pursue them. For they all point to passages in other works where there is *no evasion*, where the sense of sterility or the sense of dread comes to a full and terrible consciousness. For instance, Eliot's lines point to the terrible words of the Old Testament prophets, reminding Israel that the day of the Lord will be a day of unmitigated wrath. They echo the sickening portrayal of old age in the book of Ecclesiastes. They refer to Baudelaire's horrible vision of the nightmare city, and to the primitive belief that no crops would grow unless the fertility god were first killed, hacked to pieces, and buried in the ground. The lines in German are from Wagner's opera *Tristan und Isolde,* in which the power of love destroys everything. In the words "*Oed' und leer das Meer,*" a servant tells the dying Tristan that the sea is empty and that Isolde does not approach. "I was neither/Living nor dead" are Dante's words for describing his paralyzed terror at the bottom of hell, when he finally beholds Satan face to face. In all these passages, the sense of sterility or the sense of dread has come to a full and imaginatively satisfying expression.

These passages, however, are all to be found in *other* books, in *other* languages, in the consciousness of *other* ages. That, as I take it, is Eliot's point. The allusions only reinforce what the listening ear has already fully discovered for itself through the verbal impact of the lines—that in *this* poem and *this* world the dread of life causes all craving for life to be numbed and buried. To try to import the clarity of these other books into our reading of Eliot's verse is to lose touch with the actual poetic impact of his lines. Unlike his poems of 1920, *The Waste Land* does not set up a contrast between the past and the present for the listening ear. There is no condemnation of the evasiveness presented here, and to impute such an attitude to the poem is to assume that whenever people cling to sterility they are naturally to be reprimanded. But Eliot has here passed beyond the sheer revulsion of his earlier work. He does not want to scold the modern world for its sterility. He wants to penetrate to the dread which holds people in this misery, and to explore the domains of immediacy which foster that dread. The poem, in other words, begins at a point that impulsive reformers and outraged humanists never reach. Primarily because Eliot here seeks to understand and not to condemn, he is able to commit himself to exploring the actual music of city speech, without being impelled to create another poetic language alongside of it. In his diction he has a patience with the language of living voices that does not appear in his earlier work.

V.

The second section of the poem shows a marked increase in surface clarity. Instead of a jumble of fragments, we are given two carefully developed scenes, each of which is dominated by the voice and mood of a single speaking character. Even more important, both parts of the section reflect the same fundamental attitude, a protest against sterility, a cry for life, specifically in the relationship between men and women. The poetry now does what the frustrated reader wanted it to do all through the first section, not just to reflect the stultifying wasteland of the city, but to use its musical capacities to say No to this wasteland.

The section opens in a woman's lavish boudoir, where her jewels, her perfume, her chair, and mirror are all elaborately described. The language is as extreme in its poetic ornateness as the lines in the preceding section were flat and bare. The richness, however, belongs only to the scene. It does not serve to reflect the lives of the people who inhabit the room. When the verse moves into focus upon the woman herself and upon the man—presumably her husband—whose approaching foot-steps "shuffle" on the stairs, the lines become harsh and bitter. The reader again meets the same collapse of richness as filled the opening section, and again feels the desire to protest. This time the poetry itself gives voice to his feeling. We hear the woman complaining to her husband against the way in which all life has gone out of their marriage.

> "My nerves are bad to-night. Yes, bad. Stay
>   with me.
> "Speak to me. Why do you never speak. Speak.
> "What are you thinking of? What
>   thinking? What?
> "I never know what you are thinking. Think."

The man's response is a shock. He says nothing to his wife, but only withdraws, as it were, into a despair of his own.

> I think we are in rats' alley
> Where the dead men lost their bones.

She wants some kind of refreshing contact with this man, who, as her husband, is supposed to be for her a source of life, vivifying and fructifying her. All he can do is to think of the finality of death, and therefore the ultimate sterility of all action. The scene continues in this fashion. Before her groping effort to find him and to feel his vital presence, he is closed off from her by this paralyzing thought of death. If death alone rules, what is the point of striving for life or love? What is the point of doing anything but pursuing the pointless routine and playing irrelevant games until the end comes?

> "What shall we do to-morrow?
> "What shall we ever do?"
> The hot water at ten.
> And if it rains, a closed car at four.
> And we shall play a game of chess,
> Pressing lidless eyes and waiting for a knock upon
> the door.

In the thoughts of the husband, a new and decisive music has entered into the poem. The empty city chatter, the flowery description of the boudoir, and even the woman's cry of protest all recede into the background. The sense of death now dominates the listening ear. It is presented as the hidden factor behind all those lifeless evasions that seemed so exasperating in Section I. The people who take baths and avoid rain and make noises at each other over coffee may do so only because they have no illusions. Like the husband in this scene, they simply know that they are not truly alive and that there is no such thing as "Life." For the first time in the poem, a perception has emerged that demands genuine metaphors ("pressing lidless eyes") and a deliberately controlled rhythm. It is a perception that merits poetry. But—and this is the decisive point—this perception is not imported into the situation by means of some artificial poetic music fabricated by the author. It has emerged from *within* the matrix of city speech, the author working only to bring it into focus.

The other scene in this section also expresses and then undercuts protest. We are in a London pub at closing time. A working woman is recounting how she rebuked a friend of hers for not looking her best and getting her ugly teeth replaced in preparation for her husband's return from the army.

> He'll want to know what you done with that
>   money he gave you
> To get yourself some teeth. He did, I was there.
> You have them all out, Lil, and get a nice set,
> He said, I swear, I can't bear to look at you.
> And no more can't I, I said, and think of poor
>   Albert,
> He's been in the army four years, he wants a
>   good time,
> And if you don't give it him, there's others will,
>   I said.
> Oh is there, she said. Something o' that, I said.
> Then I'll know who to thank, she said, and give
>   me a straight look.

We are a long way from the boudoir in speech mannerisms, but we hear the same protest against a lifeless marriage. The speaker, an unmarried woman herself probably, is indignant that Lil has not seen her husband's coming as a kind of restoration of her life. Albert, the speaker believes, should be a principle of vitality to his wife, and if she won't recognize it "there's others will, I said."

As the account continues, however, we suddenly discover what kind of vitality Lil has already received from Albert.

> You ought to be ashamed, I said, to look so
>   antique.
> (And her only thirty-one.)
> I can't help it, she said, pulling a long face,
> It's them pills I took, to bring it off, she said.

> (She's had five already, and nearly died of
>   young George.)
> The chemist said it would be all right, but I've
>   never been the same.

For Lil the procreative vitality has proved nearly fatal. Far from being a source of life, it has become a source of death. It not only nearly killed her at one point, but by its very fruitfulness has crushed her with the care of five children, a burden she has had to carry alone in her husband's absence. In trying to avoid the ravages of this procreative life, she has only brought on herself some kind of organic illness. From her viewpoint, her husband's return can hardly be a source of joy.

Here, as in the scene in the boudoir, the threat of death serves to undercut the atmosphere of protest. But Eliot does not depend simply on this disclosure of Lil's situation to bring the sense of death before the listening ear. In her account of her clash with Lil, the speaker is continually being interrupted by the ordinary phrase with which London pubkeepers announced the approach of closing time: "Hurry up, please. It's time." As Eliot uses this line, however, it is far from ordinary. It is set apart in block letters, without punctuation, as if it came from outside the scene. Its slow, spondaic rhythm disrupts the impulsive flow of chatter from the woman, like an ominous voice off stage. Further still, it appears so soon after the reference to pressing lidless eyes and waiting for a knock upon the door that the ear inevitably makes a connection between them. In this line, then, the reader not only hears the ordinary meaning, but he also has the vague impression that these are the words of death itself, knocking and calling the soul away. For the ear and eye, they keep mocking the speaker's protest for a more enthusiastic pursuit of life. They keep reminding the ear of the despairing knowledge that the husband voiced in the previous scene: "I think we are in rats' alley/Where the dead men lost their bones."

At the end of this second section, the atmosphere of frustrated protest collapses. The working woman turns away from the torments of children, decay, betrayal, and abortion, and enjoys the memory of a nice hot dinner. But the reader no longer takes this evasion seriously. For his listening ear there can be no return to the evasiveness of the opening section of the poem. As long as he does not have to think about the ever present power of death, as long as he remains in the world of conventional poetry where life is simply good and exaltation is simply pleasurable, he can be angry at the husband who does not speak in a vivifying way to his wife, or at the wife who does not beautify herself for her husband's home-coming. Perhaps, if he really believed in love and life, his baffled exasperation would drive him to insanity, like Ophelia in Shakespeare's *Hamlet*, or to attempted suicide like Philomel, or to real suicide, like Cleopatra in Shakespeare's play or Dido in Vergil's *Aeneid*. But these responses, to which Eliot refers in his notes, belong in other books. Here all protest is undercut by the knowledge of the power of death—first as a great embracing fatality, and then as an insidious trap that surprises a person along whatever life-giving road he tries to follow. People may fail to be faithful to the power of life, but more important is the way in which the power of life fails to be faithful to them. In the knowledge of that betrayal, human failures cease to matter. Now, at the conclusion of this second section of the poem, even the most casual surface detail becomes an ironic reminder of this ultimate betrayal.

> HURRY UP PLEASE IT'S TIME
> HURRY UP PLEASE IT'S TIME
> Goonight Bill. Goonight Lou. Goonight May.
>   Goonight.
> Ta ta. Goonight. Goonight.
> Good night, ladies, good night, sweet ladies,
>   good night, good night.

Is this the usual closing time in any pub on any night? Or is this a grotesque parody of the last and final good-by that hangs over all things?

VI.

The second section shows the collapse of all protests and hopes in the thought of death. In the third section this despair becomes the operating basis of human life. We have reached the heart of the poem.

The characters who are now presented to us have passed beyond all evasions and protests, even beyond disillusion. They have come to expect nothing at all from their existence. Their daily routine between office and apartment has no order or rhythm. It is meaningless clutter. Dirty breakfast dishes still cover the table at supper-time. Stray clothes are tossed on the divan during the day; a tired body is tossed on it at night. Above all, sexuality has become completely separated from love and life. It does not bring refreshment, and does not release any creative vitality. It is thought of simply as a diversion, or a compulsive mechanical habit. A foreign merchant seeks a homosexual alliance for the weekend. A typist, having eaten a dreary supper from tin cans, tired from the day's work, submits listlessly to the sexual assaults of a casual acquaintance. People look upon each other as mere objects, or as convenient instruments of their biological needs. But no one voices a protest. The typist does not cry out to her caller, "My nerves are bad tonight. Yes, bad. Stay with me./Speak to me. Why do you never speak." These two people are meaningless to each other, and she has no idea that the situation could possibly be different.

> She turns and looks a moment in the glass,
> Hardly aware of her departed lover;
> Her brain allows one half-formed thought to pass:
> "Well now that's done: and I'm glad it's over."
> When lovely woman stoops to folly and
> Paces about her room again, alone,
> She smoothes her hair with automatic hand,
> And puts a record on the gramophone.

This section imposes a double shock upon the reader, first by giving a direct account of degraded sexuality, and second by letting none of the characters share the revulsion that he feels. He is offended by what they do, but even more by their indifferent acceptance of what they do. The task for the poetry is to carry the reader through and beyond his own attitude of shock, to bring him to the point where he can hear of these things and not rise in protest, where he, too, like the characters, has become conditioned to the sickening sterility. In order to achieve this end, the verse carries his ear through three kinds of verbal music.

There is first an ugly vision of a world where death is king. All people and their trash have disappeared. Only their bones remain—and rats creeping through the slime. The sense of waste is in the center of the stage, but it is not accepted. The poetry strains with excessively revulsive images, as if, in exasperated protest, it wanted to make the ugliness as sickening as possible. It also intersperses a few lines of quiet beauty—"Sweet Thames, run softly till I end my song"—which highlight by contrast the prevailing foulness. In their emotional tone, these lines want to discredit and repudiate the scene that they present. They pick up the protesting attitude of Section II. They reflect the tone and style that Eliot developed in his poems of 1920. The speaking voice, one feels, is filled with nothing but revulsion.

This effortfully revulsive speech soon disappears, however. The scene of fornication in the typist's apartment is presented with ruthless directness. The lines do not protest; they describe. The reading imagination finds no crevice in which to dream of how this might be different, and hears no hint in the words that it should be different. Most important of all, the whole incident is presented to the reader through the eyes of the blind Tiresias, a prophet in ancient Greek mythology. For him, this sterile fornication is not an abnormal incident, from which his mind can turn away by thinking of how people "usually" pursue their erotic conduct. This, he declares, is what has always happened. This has been part of human existence since the dawn of history.

> And I Tiresias have foresuffered all
> Enacted on this same divan or bed;

> I who have sat by Thebes below the wall
> And walked among the lowest of the dead.

Finally, after this heavy weight of realism, there follow two stanzas of genuinely lyrical verse.

> The river sweats
> Oil and tar
> The barges drift
> With the turning tide
> Red sails
> Wide
> To leeward, swing on the heavy spar.

For the first time in the whole poem, the lines deal with the kind of loveliness that, before Eliot, was generally taken to be the only proper subject matter for poetry. The effect of this upon the listening ear, however, is not at all a sense of refreshing exaltation. For the beauty we meet is only that of mandolins and old churches, of oil and tar on the river, of surface pageantry from the age of Queen Elizabeth. It does not grip the ear with any serious promise of life. It does not claim to offer any genuine fulfillment. The dalliance between Queen Elizabeth and Robert Leicester that it mentions was just as sterile as that between the typist and the clerk, even though it had the benefit of bright colors, fresh breezes, and pealing bells.

These lyrics do provide relief from the ugly realism, but only with flashes of surface splendor. They make no pretence of releasing the vitalities of life. To the listening ear, therefore, they confirm the impression that the world in its basic substance is sterile trash.

> The barges wash
> Drifting logs
> Down Greenwich reach
> Past the Isle of Dogs.
> > Weialala leia
> > Wallala leialala.

We have reached the point where even beauty makes no effort to suppress the essential emptiness of the world on which it shines.

The ear is now ready to return to an encounter with degraded sexuality, without expecting to hear any protest. In quick succession three girls speak of their meaningless seductions by the river, one "supine on the floor of a narrow canoe," another indifferent to the fatuous remorse of her companion.

> "After the event
> He wept. He promised 'a new start.'
> I made no comment. What should I resent?"

There is no protest here, no revulsion. And the reading imagination itself shares in this passive acceptance. It has passed through and beyond the point of expecting anything else. As far as the poem has actualized a world to our listening ear, this is simply the way things are.

The significant thing about this third section of the poem is that it represents for Eliot a genuine poetic advance beyond the orientation of his poems of 1920. He succeeds in carrying his language beyond the stage of revulsion, beyond the jarring contrast between splendid past and squalid present. He no longer has to vitalize his lines with the dynamic of outraged protest. He does not have to inspire his verse with the energy of nausea, which was all that his predecessors could do with the city. He does not have to create some other, more "poetic" language to stand in judgment upon sordid city speech.

Poetically this means that he can give himself to the consciousness and language of city existence without any reservations. He does not find that the empty rhythmless speech there is an obstacle. On the contrary, it has its own poetic values, which he can explore. He has succeeded in making the city, just as it is, a domain for poetry. And he has done this by disengaging poetry completely from any hope of exaltation, and identifying it wholly with a world of *suffering*.

VII.

The poem, however, is not over. This passage beyond evasion and protest to despairing acceptance has not exhausted the major tones that we hear in city speech or the chief kinds of impact made by urban immediacy. At the very end of Section III we encounter a new note: "O Lord Thou pluckest me out/O Lord Thou pluckest."

In their context, these words carry no specific religious impact. They do not actualize the sense of some real Lord who acts and saves. They have the character of a blind, despairing cry for *escape*, directed toward any power, known or unknown, that might happen to respond. They are the words of the man who has no more illusions about the world around him, and who has nowhere to go for life but into some blank elsewhere.

Section IV—"Death by Water"—carries out this music of escape. It is a stanza about Phlebas the Phoenician, who has drowned at sea and who in death has found release from the intolerable burdens of life.

> Phlebas the Phoenician, a fortnight dead,
> Forgot the cry of gulls, and the deep sea swell
> And the profit and loss.

The lines here become soft and liquid. They seem moved by some deep rhythm from beyond the spasmodic hurry of human busyness. Phlebas no longer tosses on the surface among waves and gulls. He sinks into a current under the sea, into a time not our time, a time older than the time of chronometers.

But is this the desired end? Is this an endless tranquility, a perpetual and fulfilling rest? By some curious twist, as the lines proceed they begin to convey the impression, not of peace, but of destruction. The undersea current did not rock Phlebas in blissful repose. It "picked his bones in whispers." He was not freed from time and stress. "As he rose and fell/He passed the stages of his age and youth/Entering the whirlpool." The listening ear cannot identify this whirlpool image with any fact or reference in the objective world. It functions wholly within this stanza, suggesting that this death was not a sleep for Phlebas, but a merciless re-experience of his whole existence leading him to some terrible cataclysm. This simply re-echoes the note of dread, and reminds the ear of Section I: that the self does not surrender to death or any other mystery without an agony of terror. In any case these lines do not fulfill the promise of escape and peace that seems to lie in their deep rhythm. In some obscure way they deprive us of the satisfaction we expected. In other books, of course, such as the New Testament, death by water is indeed a redemption, not by giving eternal sleep, but by bringing forth a new life through the death of the old. (Rom. 6:3.) In this stanza, however, Phlebas' sea-swallowed corpse is only a negation. It does not promise relief; it only proves the folly of seeking life. It mocks and judges all those "who turn the wheel and look to windward."

This leads into the fifth and final section of the poem, in which the element of the dreadful comes into the foreground. Up to this point, we have seen fear working in a number of the characters, especially in Section I, but we have not had actualized the kind of world that provokes that fear. Instead we have encountered worlds that foster other attitudes, such as protest, or despair, or escape. The decisive fact in all these perspectives is the *collapse* of life. Suffering of one kind or another arises because life fails to be fruitful. What enters the poem in this final section, however, is active evil. Men do not die simply because the power of life is weak and constantly fails through its own impotence. They are crushed by counter-realities of greater power. In other words, the world in its immediate impact is not just empty of life, but is full of the *positive* power of death. It has become a demonic realm. The forces that rule it and that are always secretly working behind its normal façade are forces of sheer destruction.

This way of experiencing the world pervades the consciousness and language of all people in modern cities. There is everywhere an undertone of fear, which keeps rising to the surface of voices and then subsiding. It is as if people were constantly watching for some ferocity to break out upon them from the swirling crowds or the speeding cars or the international crisis.

The final section of the poem brings this demonic world into focus. It presents a series of scenes in which physical life and social life and mental sanity are all subjected to some crushing pressure. Nature is not barren. It has become a terrific energy of suffocating heat, shriveling up all things. Human beings even cease to be convenient instruments for each other, much less objects of love. No one here suffers from loneliness or cries out for companionship. There are only sullen faces sneering at each other. The city is unreal, not, as in Section I, because it is hidden under a brown fog, where each man fixes his eyes before his feet, but because it bursts apart in the violet air before barbaric hordes. Individuals become nightmare figures—bats with baby faces and a woman fiddling whisper music on her hair. There is even a chapel here, surrounded by open graves and filled with the wind.

In this panorama, Eliot has actualized the kind of world immediately present to the mind when it is gripped by the feeling of dread. Elements from earlier parts of the poem have become terrifying. Death is not the mere absence of life, nor drought the absence of water, nor alienation the absence of love. These conditions are the result of active dynamic forces. "Death" means "to be killed"; "dryness" means "to be withered"; "isolation" means "to be hated."

The poetry of this section still remains close to the manner and vocabulary of city speech and still works with the musical tones heard in city voices. But it has now reached the final and most elusive level of urban suffering. We have come a long way from the opening stanza, where rain meant only inconvenience and where every immanent vitality was a disturbance that could easily be avoided. Now all the things to which men normally turn for ordinary life—nature, human society, the house of worship—are felt to be creatures of destruction.

VIII.

At the conclusion of the poem, after this long progression through different levels of waste and death, the scene is finally touched by life-giving rain. Refreshment is at hand.

This, however, applies only to the scene and not to the poetry. For the ear, which responds to the immediate impact of the lines, nothing happens. There is no break-through into joy and peace, no comment of soaring ecstasy. Using a story from the sacred writings of the Hindus, Eliot actualizes the approach of life as booming thunder. The thunder announces the secret of human fulfillment, but all that strikes the ear is an ominous and inscrutable *Da*. For Eliot gives us the thunder's message in three Sanskrit words—*Datta, Dayadhvam, Damyatta*. In the notes, these are roughly translated as "Give, sympathize, control," but in the moment of reading, they convey nothing to the ear but a rather threatening sound. As happened before in the poem, the reading imagination is dismayed just when it expects to be exalted. Moreover, as the verse responds to the thunder's words, all that we hear is an anguished or melancholic despair. *Datta?* "Give"? The only time we ever gave ourselves was in that first moment of sexual abandon. *Dayadhvam?* "Sympathize"? How can we sympathize, when each of us is locked in the private solitariness of his own self? *Damyatta?* "Control"? Control and direction from whom? In the world that we know, there are no expert life-giving hands into whose control we can confidently surrender ourselves. With that, the last lines of the poem degenerate for the ear into a jumble of quotations in four languages. It ends with an unintelligible benediction, a three-fold repetition of the Sanskrit word for "peace."

Even here, then, Eliot remains faithful to the limits of his medium. He does not try to import a bit of uplift into his verse. He does not try to have his cake and eat it too, breaking with the old tradition of exalted poetry, and yet at the end getting in a bit of exaltation of his own. He has chosen to work within the resonances of living city speech and to recover the impact of immediacy that absorbs the city consciousness. To the ear this language betrays the absence of everything vital and rhythmically exalting. It expresses many levels of agony—that is its positive content which poetry can articulate—but it knows no appeasement for this agony. The conclusion of *The Waste Land* simply gives decisive expression to what the reader has found to be true from the beginning: where this city language is spoken the only growth or increase of perception is toward deeper levels of suffering. The verbal actualization of joy, even of the joy that lies on the farther side of suffering, belongs to other languages and therefore in other books.

IX.

Because of its use of rhythm and imaginative metaphor, poetry tends to become the language of intense experience. It has a natural momentum in this direction. This momentum was fully exploited by the poetry that prevailed before Eliot. As a result, a profound contrast developed between the actual speech of city people and the soaring resonances of this poetry. In the day-to-day routine of a modern metropolis, the speaking voice did not have many occasions to express itself with rhythmic vibrancy. Writers discovered that they had to withdraw into the woods, or into the depths of the human heart, or at least into an attitude of revulsion, if they wanted to sustain their poetry at a maximal level. They were forced to develop an artificial language with a far richer music than could be heard in the streets or offices of the city. On the other hand, if any of them had not wanted to withdraw, then they would have had to remove every desire for maximal poetry from their own ears and imagination, accepting the actualities of city speech and city consciousness as they found them, and remaining within the limits of this urban realm.

This latter was the road that Eliot followed in *The Waste Land*. Confronted by the opposition between city speech and maximal poetry, he stopped trying to draw some kind of poetic intensity out of the city. He gave his verse over to city speech, and turned his back on every kind of maximal poetry.

In practice, this meant that he developed what could at that time only sound like an offensively "unpoetic" poetry, a poetry devoid of all those intensities and melodious sounds that had become identified with poetic discourse. He explained his poetic aims precisely in these terms.

> To write poetry which should be essentially poetry, with nothing poetic about it, poetry standing naked in its bare bones, or poetry so transparent that we should not see the poetry, but that which we are meant to see through the poetry, poetry so transparent that in reading it we are intent on what the poem *points at*, and not on the poetry, this seems to me the thing to try for. To get *beyond poetry*, as Beethoven, in his later works, strove to get *beyond music*.[6]

This "not seeing" the poetry is just a negative way of saying that what the poet should use is ordinary speech, speech which belongs so fully to the flow of ordinary life that it does not call attention to itself when it strikes the ear.

But why should a reader want "unpoetic" poetry? What new enhancement does he find, to compensate for the loss of maximal intensity? Has he simply thrown away the lilt of song for a dry verse that could just as well be put in prose? What he gains is a heightened sense of his own everyday language, of the speech that he himself constantly uses and constantly hears. He becomes more aware of the perceptions that determine the tone and vibrancy of his own voice. He discovers and enjoys the poetic possibilities that lie in his own conversation. Eliot has emphasized this value for poetry.

> No poetry, of course, is ever exactly the same speech that the poet talks and hears: but it has to be in such a relation to the speech of his time that the listener or reader can say 'that is how I should talk if I could talk poetry'. This is the reason why the best contemporary poetry can give us a feeling of excitement and a sense of fulfilment different from any sentiment aroused by even very much greater poetry of a past age.[7]

For poetry that seeks to achieve a maximum of intensity, nothing is more alien than the style of ordinary speech. An exceptional level of experience requires an exceptional kind of language, and anything prosaic automatically spoils the desired effect. On the other hand, for poetry which follows the direction that Eliot sketches here and which wants to give the reader the excitement of hearing a heightening of his own daily speech, the great danger is artificiality. Any verse that uses a vocabulary and idiom peculiar to itself and not shared by living speech automatically becomes incapable of giving this excitement. It may be unusually intense, but it is not an intensification of what actual people are saying to each other. In order to reach this latter goal, poetry must approach—and not withdraw from—the unpoetic style of ordinary speech. It must avoid every trace of artificiality, even at the risk of becoming prosaic.

This was the direction that Eliot took in *The Waste Land*. The poem has no moment when the words and the consciousness are carried to extraordinary levels. It is never far from the language of prose. What it sacrifices in intensity, however, it gains in relevance. It does at least give some heightening to the whole realm of words and perceptions that actually envelop the ordinary person.

This revolution in poetic intention is one aspect of Eliot's achievement in *The Waste Land*. He helped re-establish the connection between poetry and daily speech. But this change did not simply involve a rejection of "poetic" language in favor of ordinary language. Each of these languages was itself the voice of a fundamental human attitude, so that when a poet adopted either language as his medium, he was also identifying himself with the attitude that generated it. This matter of fundamental attitude is what makes the poetry of *The Waste Land* important for the Christian community.

As this poem makes its immediate impact on the ear, we can say that it presents a series of *suffering* voices, instead of the joyful voices which could be heard in the poetic style that prevailed earlier. If we listen to this poem, not so much as the statement of some private ideas that the poet has fashioned inside his head, but as a careful realization of various tones of voice that his ear has heard on the city streets, then the city, we find, is a place where men do not often and do not naturally speak with joy. Judging primarily by the general emotional tenor of their speaking voices, we must say that on any given day they do not expect to meet an exhilarating refreshment, which will lift them above themselves. Normally their voices seem to reflect only different kinds of suffering, or, if this word is too strong, different levels of dissatisfaction, different kinds of boredom or loneliness or irritation or fatigue or panic. This peculiar fact about the modern city does not reveal itself only in Eliot's verse, of course. We find the same atmosphere of dissatisfaction in the great volume of urban poetry that has appeared in recent decades, in the serious plays and novels about city life, and in the endless flow of newspaper headlines. Even the word "realism" has come to mean an unflinching portrayal of human misery, as if no one could attain the "reality" of modern existence until he had faced up to its unrelieved suffering.

Since there are all kinds and ways of suffering, it is important to note that the suffering heard in city speech and brought into special focus in *The Waste Land* has two distinctive features. First of all, dissatisfaction is not one of the possibilities that may or may not befall a person, depending on how his situation develops. It is a product, not so much of his special circumstances, as of the world itself. It arises from the way in which the whole universe of faces, things, and responsibilities grates upon him. Regardless of what particular happenings occur, the world as such, in any and all of its shapes, seems to exasperate the human spirit in some way. Even when events prove fulfilling in some specific and limited way, they are only incidental exceptions against an oppressive background. They do not transform the city into a life-giving environment. They do not relieve the weight of its nerve-racking pressures, or the scope of its disorder and social emptiness. There seems to be some fundamental deficiency, or inhumanity, in the the world as such, without regard to particular circumstances.

City voices often betray this sense of inevitable suffering, as if nothing else could ever be expected. A person in the city may constantly protest against this or that irritation, against the weather or the politicians, and he may somehow narcotize this or that pain. Yet he has no illusions about expecting anything different. When the corrupt political machine is turned out of office, he does not begin speaking in a voice alive with anticipation. *The Waste Land* is particularly successful in actualizing this undertone of hopelessness in city speech.

The other feature of this urban suffering is that it gives those who endure it no sense of dignity. They do not think of themselves as struggling heroically against evil, or as taking part in some momentous drama, or as being crushed by some impressive enemy. It is more like the agony described by Marlowe, one of the characters in Conrad's *Heart of Darkness*.

> I have wrestled with death. It is the most unexciting contest you can imagine. It takes place in an impalpable grayness, with nothing underfoot, with nothing around, without spectators, without clamour, without glory, without the great desire of victory, without the great fear of defeat, in a sickly atmosphere of tepid scepticism, without much belief in your own right, and still less in that of your adversary.[8]

The exasperations of city life have this same quality. They do not provide a basis for significant action or personal enhancement. They even infect the human struggle against them with their own triviality.

It should now be clear what a revolution in *expectations* must occur, when any poet or reader lets his ear be limited to the music of actual city speech. This not only means that he gives up the language and imagery of exaltation—the quiet woods and rolling hills, the soft vowel sounds and melodious rhythms. It also means that he has removed even the faintest expectation for this fulfillment from his listening ear. He does not keep wishing secretly for richer music, and he does not become angry that city speech keeps disappointing him. He even gets beyond the point where the city revolts him, since he feels revulsion only toward that which he expected to be glorious. He genuinely accepts this city language as his medium, and in that act also accepts the distinctive attitude toward suffering that pervades its tones.

Now we have reached the heart of the impasse between city speech and the poetry of exaltation. This opposition is not just a matter of locale or rhythm or imagery. It involves the kind of emotional expectations that any speaking voice arouses in an ear that hears it. In the city frustration and disorder are the inescapable stuff of life. People there look forward at most to moments of temporary relief—to a vacation, to a good book, to one night of real sleep. This sense of the inevitability of suffering is the tonal quality that the older poetry of exaltation could never catch. By its rhythms and attitudes, it always suggested a world where joy was concretely possible, and therefore always stood opposed to the emotional horizons of city speech.

If *The Waste Land* stands out as the first major poem in English to absorb the living language of the modern city, this is because it accepts the dry, undramatic, uninspiring city attitude toward inevitable suffering. It does not keep titillating the reader with other, more satisfying possibilities. It does not keep glancing into the distance for some hypothetical fulfillment. It moves, and conveys an expectation of moving, only from one suffering to another. It fully identifies itself with a joyless tone of voice, so that even the final life-giving appearance of rain does not disrupt this basic tone, and does not initiate a new music of hope. The structure of the poem certainly suggests that life, if it is to be found at all, will appear only after a person has passed in and through the whole gamut of city suffering. It will not be found in flight from suffering. The poem itself, however, keeps to the tone of real city speech, and does not try to actualize this possible encounter with life. We can say that in *The Waste Land* Eliot has disciplined his ear to stay close to the speech of real city people. Yet we must not forget that this poetic discipline actually involves a discipline of his emotional expectations.

Needless to say, many commentators on *The Waste Land* have not been able to follow Eliot through this emotional revolution. Confronted with city ugliness, they can conceive of no other poetic reaction but one of protest and revulsion. They cannot imagine a spiritual state in which the self has actually given up all dreams of exaltation, and really lives in a gray world of perpetual frustration. They have not let the peculiar joyless realism of city life control their self-conscious attitudes. *The Waste Land*, they insist, is a cry *against* the waste of modern life, *against* the hopelessness in city voices, *against* the irreligion of our secularized culture. It proclaims the need for some meaningful myth or some religious revival, they say. These readers fail to appreciate how radical a revolution Eliot achieved in this poem. They do not hear the verse's complete and unreserved identification with city speech and city suffering, its inner acceptance of city grime. Poetically and emotionally, they are still in the nineteenth century, where good things exalt us, ugly things revolt us, and everything shakes us *intensely*. They are not aware that it is precisely this ideal of intensity which the poem has abandoned, either intense hope or intense disappointment, and which it has abandoned in view of the sense of inescapable suffering that pervades city speech.

X.

This peculiar attitude toward suffering gives the poem some importance for the Christian community. This community represents, among other things, a distinctive language realm, with its own words and its own fashions in style and attitude. We might say that in the English-speaking world during the last century the tone of Christian language has often sounded exactly like the prevailing poetry of exaltation. That is, it has a way of arousing high emotional expectations. It gives the impression that Christianity has its value in inspiring men here and now with some kind of exalted feeling. It somehow takes them away from, or minimizes the impact of, or even initiates improvements in the ugly urban world around them. It is supposed to make our present neighbors more lovable and our present life more meaningful.

On the Protestant side, the emphasis was "evangelical." Jesus Christ was the "good news" (*evaggelion* in Greek), and he should be presented as someone who enriches human life. In

Christ, it was said, you personally shall find a new meaning for existence, a new basis for action, a new capacity for love. There was something self-enhancing about being a Christian. The tone and style of much Protestant language made it sound as if, once a person becomes a Christian, then everything takes on a new and exhilarating significance. On the Roman Catholic side, the emphasis was less on the enhancement of the self and more on the immovable and tranquilizing stability of the Church. The Church, it was said, is undivided and unchanging from generation to generation. She has been given the truth, through which any person may see the order of God's plan in all things. There are laws and regulations for every human action. There are revealed truths for every human doubt. In spite of the apparent upheaval of modern life, the person who belongs to the Church can see around him a stable, law-governed world.

The effect of both this Protestant and this Roman Catholic emphasis was the same. It placed the Christian community and the Christian life over against suffering. It gave the impression that insofar as a man was a Christian he was somehow disengaged from the sufferings that besieged his age. If he was a Protestant, his divine faith was supposed to keep him immune from all the pitfalls of personal despair, and to motivate him to serve his neighbor devotedly. If he was a Roman Catholic, his divine Church was supposed to remove the apparent disorder of the human world and to give him a clear-cut moral code for every situation. What minister would not boldly promise the members of his congregation that their faith in God would help them find more meaning in their marriage? What priest would not tell his flock exactly the sins that they would find on the beaches in summertime and exactly the countermeasures that they should take? Everywhere the Christian community spoke as if it lived in the midst of inspiring faith, eager love, and obvious law; as if, in its own interior life, it had no problem with loneliness or confusion; as if the dull misery of city people and the sharp anguish of Christ in Gethsemane were equally foreign to its religious vitality.

We can certainly understand why it followed this course. Confronted by the growing scepticism and disbelief of modern times, it thought to counter with a posture of bold assurance. It set up an opposition between the exalted realm of faith and the messy realm of secular modernity, hoping thereby to encourage people to turn from the latter and seek the former. It wanted to match the self-confidence of secularism with its own God-confidence, and to expose the inner miseries of modern man by the depths of its own security.

In all of this the Christian community proved to be disastrously wrong. Modernity—with its sense of God's absence and its struggle against the enormous weight of the world—turned out not to be a viewpoint or an interpretation that a man "adopted" by some will of his own and that he could drop whenever he saw fit. It proved to be an enveloping atmosphere in which he lived. He could no more leave it at will than he could jump out of his skin. A Catholic might read all the books in his bishop's library on moral principles and natural order, but he would still experience the walk across a busy street as an immersion in violent disorder. A Protestant might sincerely believe that he is to serve his neighbors as individual persons, but he would still feel the impersonal, thing-like impact of voices on the telephone or faces at the committee meeting. Becoming a Christian did not at all have the effect of making the city a more tranquil or more human place to work, did not give the individual a sense of control over his urban environment. Therefore, when people heard the Christian community making a contrast between happiness in faith and misery in the "secular" world, they could only conclude that their own workaday life, which was completely embedded in the pointless secularity of the city, was doomed. Insofar as the urban world imposed itself upon their consciousness, they could only feel cut off from the Christ of confident faith, or the Christ of intimate fellowship, or the Christ of secure law. Conversely, whatever inspiration they may have received from one of these Christs on Sunday, it seemed to have little bearing on the bleak, impersonal world of city experience.

Like the poetry of exaltation, then, the Christian community failed to take the city into itself. It only set up counter-worlds of escape, where Christ was supposed to do away with the miseries of urban chaos (let us listen to God's law!), and urban dread (let us believe in God's goodness!), and urban loneliness (let us love all of God's children!). The Christian community had nothing to say, not only to the unchurched millions whose lives were immersed in the city, but also to the city experience of its own members. It certainly could not include the empty, joyless tones of city speech within its own horizons.

This purely positive version of Christianity not only proved wrong in its analysis of modernity. It also could not be justified in terms of its own inner life. The entire testimony of the New Testament controverts the notion that in Christ men find an escape from their worldly miseries. To come into relation with Christ, to know the love and glory of God—this does not make a man more contented with his environment or more approving of his neighbors or more satisfied with himself. It has just the opposite effect. In terms of his relation to the world, it exposes the relative *unreality* of all things other than God. It shows him that he can expect neither life nor joy from these creaturely things, however impressive they may appear; that in themselves they are all ultimately sterile. In fact, their seeming goodness, far from being a straightforward blessing that he should catalogue in endless prayers of gratitude, actually confronts him with a treacherous temptation to forget God and rest in them. Further still, contact with Christ disturbs a person's relations with himself. It exposes him to himself, in his own inexhaustible perversity. It shows him that even when he stands in the presence of God's love, he still wants his own way and still seeks to cultivate his own glory.

This double disaffection with one's world and with oneself is an inescapable part of the Christian life. The Christian community is never simply turning toward God in joy and security. Each new turning toward God involves for its members a new disillusionment about their world and a new humiliating knowledge of themselves. This is the suffering of self-denial that John of the Cross saw as the substance of Christian purification. This is the humiliation on which the young Luther put such emphasis. This is the ordeal of mortification that, for Calvin, brought the element of struggle into the Christian life. This is called "mortification," he said, to remind us "that we cannot be trained to the fear of God and learn the first principles of piety, unless we are violently smitten with the sword of the spirit and annihilated, as if God were declaring that, to be ranked among his children, there must be a destruction of our ordinary nature." [9]

If Christ does not remove men from their inner suffering, if he works to destroy and not to enhance their ordinary natures, and thus to lead them into miseries that they have never known before, he does this only for the sake of their restoration and exaltation. Suffering is not simply an external irritant, so often discussed in terms of the "problem of suffering." It is a process of inner change and transformation through which a man passes toward life. The destruction of his self-indulgent love for the world, for people, and for himself has a restorative effect. The old man in him dies that a new man may be born. He dies in Christ, so that he also may rise with Christ. His corrupt love is destroyed only in order that a freer, God-centered love for these same things may be re-created in him.

This assurance that he is broken for the sake of his exaltation enables him to assent to the destruction of his old self and to the shredding away of all his garments of pride. It does not, however, reduce the agony of his destruction. The fact that he looks forward to the fullness of life does not make the actual experience of humiliation any sweeter, or the concrete shock of disillusion any less bitter. "Be wretched and mourn and weep," James wrote to his fellow Christians (James 4:9), about the process of purifying their hearts. "Let your laughter be turned to mourning and your joy to dejection. Humble yourselves before the Lord and he will exalt you." This is a hard, dry, unsatisfying suffering. It does not have the effect of making a man a hero in his own eyes, as if he were some champion of God, called upon to carry forward the holy cause. It does not console him with secret flutterings of self-importance. He—and all people and things around him—are now caught up in the overflowing richness of God's grace, and yet they are thereby exposed in their own weakness and poverty. "What have you that you did not receive?" is the searing knowledge that eats away at the old self. (I Cor. 4:7.) Furthermore this restorative suffering does not occur in some spiritual ivory tower. It takes place in a man's living engagement with the world around him, in and through all the concrete frustrations of daily life.

Whenever the Christian community tries to identify itself only with exaltation, it becomes doubly false. In the first place, it gives the false impression that Christ means simply the direct, uncomplicated, and immediate removal of suffering. As if in Christ men should feel secure and happy about themselves and each other. As if it were their Christian duty to turn their backs on every doubt and disillusion as soon as it appeared in their hearts, before it had time to dismay the deeper level of their assurance. The Christian life is always a double process, a tearing down as well as a building up, a self-annihilation as well as—or, better, for the sake of—a self-enhancement. A Christian community that only speaks confidently is false to its own inner life.

In the second place, a strictly exalted community must try to divorce whole areas of its concrete experience from its Christian existence. It must somehow ignore those situations in which things seem meaningless and empty, or in which the self becomes sickened by a sense of human degradation. In other words, it must avoid precisely those mortifying moments that may be a crucial part of God's restoring work.

The kind of revolution that we find in *The Waste Land*, then, is no less useful to the Christian community, living wholly within the momentum of God's grace, than to a secular poet who is struggling for a new verbal music. The language in which the community speaks of its Lord does not have to be always assured, always exalted, always trying to substitute happiness for misery in the hearts of people. It does not have to make the agonies of city life into projects of social reform or examples of life in unfaith. Alongside its proclamation of the good news, it can also echo these agonies within itself. In its confessions and petitions, in its expressions of faith and hope, it can absorb the joyless tones of city speech without embarrassment. Faith and hope work not only to inspire a man with confidence but also to lead him deeper into suffering. The Christian community can affirm the city in all its senseless chaos and grim inhumanity. This is a place where Christians may live, not because it offers them an arena for some life-giving achievements, but because it can dry up and burn away all the false sources of life in them. There men may feel and taste the inner barrenness of their world and themselves. This is not a pleasant truth and not the whole truth, but it is a truth that, within the concrete working of Christ's grace, may effect a healing wound.

From this point of view, Eliot's *The Waste Land* is only an instance of a kind of poetry that the Christian community must constantly read. To hear, not exalted visions, but the actual tones of living speech, to explore the dull sufferings that reign there without revulsion or evasion—this is an essential part of its life in Christ and its service to the world. It does not exist in order to remind men that a perfect life may await them in some distant elsewhere. Its proclamation is that Perfection Itself has come to stand with them in this present life, sharing their suffering and converting it into an instrument of their redemption.

Notes for Chapter Two

1. All quotations from T. S. Eliot's poetry are taken from *Collected Poems 1909–1962* (New York: Harcourt, Brace & World, Inc., 1964). By permission of the publishers.

2. T. S. Eliot, *Selected Essays* (New York: Harcourt, Brace & World, Inc., 1932), p. 341.

3. F. O. Matthiessen, *The Achievement of T. S. Eliot: An Essay on the Nature of Poetry* (3d ed.; New York: Oxford University Press, Inc., 1959), p. 22.

4. *Ibid.*, p. 46.

5. T. S. Eliot, "The Frontiers of Criticism," *The Sewanee Review*, LXIV (1956), pp. 533f.

6. See Matthiessen, *op. cit.*, pp. 89f.

7. T. S. Eliot, *Selected Prose*, ed. John Heyward (Harmondsworth, Middlesex, Eng.: Penguin Books, 1953), p. 58.

8. Joseph Conrad, *Heart of Darkness, and Secret Sharer* (New York: New American Library, 1950), p. 134.

9. John Calvin, *Institutes of the Christian Religion*, III, 3, 8.

Chapter Three

Country Speech: *Robert Frost*

ROBERT FROST (1875–1963) stands in sharp contrast to T. S. Eliot. He deliberately turns away from the urban world in favor of the rural country. He opens his volume of collected poems [1] with an invitation.

> I'm going out to clean the pasture spring;
> I'll only stop to rake the leaves away
> (And wait to watch the water clear, I may):
> I sha'n't be gone long. — You come too.
>
> I'm going out to fetch the little calf
> That's standing by the mother. It's so young,
> It totters when she licks it with her tongue.
> I sha'n't be gone long. — You come too.

In this invitation we are involved not only with the occupations and locale of farm life, but also with the sound values of country speech. This is a slow, quiet language. It does not have to force itself to be heard above the hum in the telephone or the noise of passing traffic. It does not have to handle the confused flood of objects that keep overwhelming the urban consciousness. It reflects a situation in which men, pursuing deliberate tasks, can yet stand still and wait for things to disclose themselves, and where personal pronouns carry the heaviest rather than the least weight ("*You* come too").

In taking this direction, Frost is obviously not interested in relating poetry to city experience and city speech. For his ear, on the contrary, the city has a tendency to empty language of its poetic substance, to transform speech into talk and talk into noise. The isolation of poetry from city life may pose a problem for poets, but it is not the only problem. As Frost himself once remarked, "As though a man who likes to live in the country is disqualified! As though a person had to live in New York to be a poet! . . . Every man's life is a wreaking of himself upon something or someone. His base of operations is a personal matter. The only thing, the big thing, for us all is attack, finding something to have to take by the throat." If some poets wish to articulate what is being obscurely said by city speech, this does not prevent other poets from exploring the domains of immediacy which city speech ignores and which may sound forth in other speech. Poets work to disclose the limits, as well as the content, of prevailing language. To that end they often bring out the power and richness of alternate speech ways.

This is the significance of Frost's rural verse. It stands opposed to the standardized mass language of the nation in a number of ways. Of particular importance is its reserve, its habit of *not* stating crucial matters directly in so many words. In this way it vividly highlights the lack of restraint in much urban discourse. City speech tends to have a presumptuous autonomy in it. It never pauses or waits for its propriety. It seizes any and everything that comes before the attention, publicizing it with forthright directness. It has a way of going on and on, not respectful of the give-and-take of interpersonal contact, but propelled by some self-contained momentum of its own. In the city, speech is less an arena where people become personally present to each other than a private energy that the isolated ego hurls out against the world. Instruments such as the telephone and radio encourage this arrogance, of course. Their very existence presumes a person's right to intrude his voice into some distant situation, without first finding out whether the circumstances there are appropriate. The verbal avalanche of college education has the same effect. If the B.A. degree means nothing else, it at least tells the world that a person has had some practice in untrammeled verbalizing.

Because Frost's verse stands completely opposed to this lack of restraint, it has special value to the Christian community. For the Christian community, with its endless "pronouncements" and perpetual sermonizing, is certainly implicated in this verbal arrogance. Indeed, it must bear a special responsibility here. When speech feels no dumbness or inner hesitation in relation to God, it can hardly be expected to show restraint in other areas.

I.

Before examining Frost's quality of reserve, we must clear away a misconception about his work that still remains fairly widespread. There is in the modern urban consciousness a deep-set "nature syndrome," implanted there by the poetry of the last century, such as we noted in the preceding chapter, and sustained today by color photography. Nature is conceived as an idyllic realm, devoid of all the violence and congestion of city existence. It allows the human spirit to relax in blissful tranquility and to flow outward into a world of beauty. The idea of being "close to nature" automatically evokes this emotional pattern. What Richard Hovey said in his poem "Spring" (1896) is said today by most people planning their summer vacations.

> I said in my heart, "I am sick of four walls and a ceiling.
> I have need of the sky.
> I have business with the grass.
> I will up and get me away where the hawk is wheeling,
> Lone and high,
> And the slow clouds go by.
> I will get me away to the waters that glass
> The clouds as they pass. . . ."

Nature means the quiet loveliness of open sky and gentle breeze, of flowering meadow and glassy pool.

Since ancient times, there has been an unbroken literary tradition that has interpreted the life of country people in terms of this natural setting. Since nature is full of peaceful beauty, and since rural folk live "close to nature," their lives must share in its tranquility, and must enjoy the pleasures of perpetual peace. Rural life has been used to body forth a kind of ideal existence, in which men have passed above their usual confusions, into the cleaner air of nature.

This idyllic view of rural life has been called the pastoral tradition, because it centered more often on the figure of the shepherd than the farmer. Pastoral poetry was very popular in England in the eighteenth, seventeenth, and sixteenth centuries (Pope, Milton, Herrick, and Spenser). It flourished in the Middle Ages. In this period poets set six ingredients as making up the ideal rural landscape: open meadows and shady trees, wandering streams and cooling breezes, bright flowers and singing birds.[2] These ingredients, however, were just as standardized in the nineteenth-century work of William Cullen Bryant or Richard Hovey as they were in the fourth-century poetry of Libanius. The idealization of rural life found its classic expression in Vergil's *Georgics* and *The Eclogues*, in which we are carried to the faraway dreamland of Arcadia. Rural people may lack the luxuries of the city, Vergil acknowledged,

> But peace secure, with no trace of discontent,
> Rich manifold harvests, ease in wide domains,
> Caverns and living lakes, cool valleys deep,
> Lowing herds, soft sleep beneath the trees—
> These never fail them. . . .[3]

And before Vergil the Greek poet Theocritus wrote pastoral verse in the third century B.C. It is not too much to say that of all the poetic genres of the ancient world, the pastoral poem ranks next to the epic in its long-range influence on western literature. After all, from the first century of the Roman empire to 1800, every single European schoolboy learned Latin, and every course in Latin began with the study of Vergil's first *Eclogue*.

For the American urban imagination, this pastoral vision has become an almost automatic reflex. Present an old-fashioned, nonmechanized rural scene, *à la* Currier and Ives, and city people will immediately picture it as a setting for idyllic life. What else can be found in the midst of old farmhouses and rolling fields but "peace secure with no trace of discontent"?

Such is the vision that many people find in Frost's poems. He is enjoyed as a modern pastoral poet, who portrays the New England countryside as an idyllic scene. His Yankee manner is thought to give a nostalgic quaintness to everything. His characters have an ennobling simplicity, surrounded by nature and sustained by companionship. They cherish berry-picking.

> It's so long since I picked I almost forget
> How we used to pick berries: we took one look around,
> Then sank out of sight like trolls underground,
> And saw nothing more of each other, or heard,
> Unless when you said I was keeping a bird
> Away from its nest, and I said it was you.[4]

It is a tranquil world of apple-picking, tree-swinging, and wall-mending, of encounters with deer and flowers and birds, of neighborly visits ("I sha'n't be gone long. — You come too") and family solidity. Even a gum-gatherer from the hills becomes part of this idyll.

> I told him this is a pleasant life
> To set your breast to the bark of trees
> That all your days are dim beneath,
> And reaching up with a little knife,
> To loose the resin and take it down
> And bring it to market when you please.[5]

If this idyllic version of Frost has made him popular in some quarters, it has also provoked violent criticism. Especially in the nineteen-thirties, when the "new" poetry of city speech was beginning to establish itself, he was attacked as the representative of old-fashioned attitudes and diction. He was accused of escapism, of refusing to enter into the sufferings and quandaries of modern man, of still clinging to remnants of the nineteenth-century world.

It must be emphasized, however, that this idyllic Frost is a complete illusion. There is no secure peace or untroubled contentment in the world of his poetry. "Mending Wall," for instance, may show the quaint rural way of repairing stone walls each spring, but it also exhibits the profound and rather terrifying chasm that can exist between neighbors. To the city commuter, looking from the outside, there may be a charming simplicity about a day spent in apple-picking. But for Frost, who probes within the experience, the day has been a constant festering of greed, and now its frustrated discontent will trouble sleep.[6] The gum-gatherer may indeed have a pleasant life in some respects, living in the dimness of the deep forest and coming to market "when you please." But Frost affirms this only after he has indicated the other, unpleasant, unfree side of this life in the forest.

> There he had built his stolen shack.
> It had to be a stolen shack
> Because of the fears of fire and loss
> That trouble the sleep of lumber folk:
> Visions of half the world burned black
> And the sun shrunken yellow in smoke.

In the poem itself, this danger and this freedom are simply set side by side, as inseparable ingredients of a single whole. It is a theme to which Frost often returns: what we live by we also die by.[7]

He has no hesitation in celebrating the moments of love and goodness. They have their validity. But he sees to it that they are not isolated. "Two Look at Two," for instance, is all on the positive side. A doe and then a buck come close to two lovers, gazing at them and then passing on, without fear. In this encounter the reconciliation of men and nature is fulfilled,

> As if the earth in one unlooked-for favor
> Had made them certain earth returned their love.

On the next page, however, Frost places a poem that presents
the other side. It has two stanzas. In the first, a woman looks up
to see her husband standing suddenly before her, back from the
war, wounded but not visibly ill. They gave him back to her
alive. Everything seemed won! In the second stanza, however,
she learns that he has been given to her only to recuperate, so
that he can go again.

> She dared no more than ask him with her eyes
> How was it with him for a second trial.
> And with his eyes he asked her not to ask.
> They had given him back to her, but not to keep.

Sometimes Frost will deliberately play upon the idyllic image
of country life, in order to shatter it in a surprising reversal. In
the early poem "Storm Fear," if you pause after the line "Ah,
no!" you will find yourself expecting one attitude and quite
unprepared for what actually develops.

> When the wind works against us in the dark,
> And pelts with snow
> The lower chamber window on the east,
> And whispers with a sort of stifled bark,
> The beast,
> 'Come out! Come out!'—
> It costs no inward struggle not to go,
> Ah, no!
> I count our strength,
> Two and a child,
> Those of us not asleep subdued to mark
> How the cold creeps as the fire dies at length,—
> How drifts are piled,
> Dooryard and road ungraded,
> Till even the comforting barn grows far away,
> And my heart owns a doubt
> Whether 'tis in us to arise with day
> And save ourselves unaided.

After the opening image of the wind as a barking dog, the line "It costs no inward struggle not to go" seems to promise a peaceful mood. It is as if the coziness of the home made it immune to the torment outside, as if the speaker felt no urge to go, because of the tranquil security surrounding him. The phrase "I count our strength," with its echo of defensive battle and siege conditions, begins the reversal, which swiftly develops with the awareness of creeping cold and helpless isolation. Instead of moving through progressive stages of relaxed indolence, in accord with the idyllic picture of rural sleep, we find ourselves carried into a terrifying apprehension of death. But this reversal is not an arbitrary trick that the author plays upon the reader. The poem is effective because the feeling of terror has been clearly indicated in the opening lines by the beast image. It is partly the reader's own fault if he does not take this seriously, and goes running instead after intimations about "no inward struggle."

In Frost's world, human relationships exist in and through all kinds of alienation. Work means ruthless antagonism as well as companionship. If the earth gives unlooked-for favors to confirm her love, she also gives ample testimony of her rage[8] and viciousness,[9] and of the blank void that awaits all her creatures.[10] Frost certainly turns away from the city and withdraws into an agrarian world that now belongs to the past. To that extent he follows the pastoral tradition. But his withdrawal has no taint of idyllicism in it. On the contrary, his concern is to penetrate and grasp the fundamental realities of concrete life, realities that operate, he believes, just as much in urban existence as elsewhere, but that are not seen there, because of the distracting clutter of superficial experience. In other words, Frost's rural world is not an end in itself, but a *medium* for achieving a heightened awareness of certain aspects of immediacy. It has clarifying value, in the service of a remarkably open and many-sided realism. It therefore works in direct opposition to all idyllic tendencies. One might say that in exploring this rural world, Frost does not withdraw from the city as an arena of human life, but only from its superficial violence and noise. He rejects the public speech heard at cocktail parties and on city streets because it partakes of this same noisy and cluttered superficiality. From his point of view, therefore, any poetry that limits itself to this city speech has unwittingly cut itself off from the actual existence of city people.

In connection with this realism in Frost, we should note that his diction plays as significant a role as his subject matter. For like Eliot, he succeeds in breaking free from the artificial rhetoric of late nineteenth-century verse. And like Eliot, he does this by completely abandoning the poetry of exaltation, and developing a poetry of common speech—in his case, the speech of country people. He risks the danger of becoming flat and prosaic, and he accepts the severe limitations of a simple vocabulary and colloquial phrasing, because he wants his perceptions to be always rooted in the common consciousness. He wants his work to bring out what men already know and feel in an incoherent way, and to be cleansed of his own private idiosyncracies.

Whatever we say about Frost's subject matter and diction, however, we must recognize that at first contact a city reader is bound to experience this poetry in idyllic terms. For one thing, it presents a world which does not have the particular frustrations that plague his urban life, and which therefore must seem to him like an escape into perfect bliss. It takes a little reading to discover that there are other kinds of frustration which this poetry explores. For another thing, Frost's colloquial style reflects the casualness and restraint of rural speech. This can easily put off the city reader who gets his news in clear-cut headlines and depends on self-dramatizing conversation for his social life. He is not prepared to rest with hints and intimations.

It is this element of restraint that we must now examine.

II.

One of Frost's most popular—and interesting—poems is "Stopping by Woods on a Snowy Evening."

Whose woods these are I think I know.
His house is in the village though;
He will not see me stopping here
To watch his woods fill up with snow.

My little horse must think it queer
To stop without a farmhouse near
Between the woods and frozen lake
The darkest evening of the year.

He gives his harness bells a shake
To ask if there is some mistake.
The only other sound's the sweep
Of easy wind and downy flake.

The woods are lovely, dark and deep
But I have promises to keep,
And miles to go before I sleep,
And miles to go before I sleep.

The poem describes how someone riding at night is gripped by the spectacle of the dark and snowy woods. The spell of the moment causes him to stop, and it holds him so strongly that only the claim of waiting obligations draws him away. But what precisely is this spell? We are given a narrative of different incidents accompanying the experience, but no direct account of the content of the experience. The pleasure—and validity—of the poem lies in the way in which it indicates this content, but does not state it.

In the first three stanzas, there is a rhythmic movement of attention away from some detail in the ordinary, social, workaday world—a house in the village, a farmhouse, the harness bells—and toward the dark and solitary scene. This movement is not normal. Through the horse, which belongs wholly to the sphere of man's work and busyness, it is twice characterized as something strange. Yet it not only keeps recurring. With each new stanza the movement becomes more complete in its withdrawal from the ordinary world. Note how the opening lines consider the woods in terms of private property and refer us to a house in the village. In the next quatrain, we are not carried to such a thoroughly social region. "A farmhouse" involves people, but it also evokes a sense of isolation. With the third stanza, human society has completely vanished and only the immediate presence of the horse still reminds us of the everyday world. The flowing progression of these verses is heightened by the rhyming scheme, in which the third line of each quatrain anticipates the rhyme that dominates the next stanza.

At this point, with the movement of imaginative withdrawal almost completed, the positive attraction of the woods comes into focus. The "sweep" of "easy wind" and "downy flake" discloses the scene to be, not just cold and isolated, but filled with a wonderfully gentle quietness. This is the blessing that draws the man away from all human society.

The last stanza stands out, not only because it reverses the previous movement of withdrawal, but also because it brings the two poles of the movement into full clarity. Its opening line is the final expression of the surrounding peace—"The woods are lovely, dark and deep." Then, by contrast with this, the man thinks of the familiar world that awaits him, the promises to be kept, and the miles to be traveled. But there is nothing warm or reassuring here. By repeating the last line, Frost conveys a sense that this world is a place of sterile and painful monotony, without fruition. He thus explains the attractiveness of the isolated woods and the difficulty in turning from them. It is not their scenic beauty, but their peace, their snow-filled darkness, the way in which they exclude the whole realm of effortful exertion. The man's conduct no longer seems queer.

The last lines do something more, however. By referring to "sleep," they indicate that another experience of dark and quiet peace awaits the man after he has finished his work. They extend the situation before us. But they do so only in the most restrained way, without indicating precisely the limits of that extension. Do the miles of journey and the sleep refer simply to what the man will do on that particular night? Or do they embrace his whole life of work and the endless sleep that will follow it? Does the emotion aroused by the deep woods extend even to a desire for death? Frost refuses to elaborate. We have here the beginnings of a metamorphosis, but it is not carried through. The encounter with the woods is on the edge of becoming something else, an experience of quite other kinds of self-obliterating rest. But the poem holds back from the achievement of a full-fledged metaphor. In this respect it can be contrasted with one of Frost's earliest lyrics, "Into My Own."

> One of my wishes is that those dark trees,
> So old and firm they scarcely show the breeze,
> Were not, as 'twere, the merest mask of gloom,
> But stretched away unto the edge of doom.
>
> I should not be withheld but that some day
> Into their vastness I should steal away,
> Fearless of ever finding open land,
> Or highway where the slow wheel pours the sand.

Here the real woods are quickly and explicitly changed into an ideal realm of dark quiet, where no straining effort can ever touch the self. The image of the highway and turning wheel are parts of this total metaphor. "Stopping by Woods" does not have any such completed transformation. Every sentence remains primarily focused upon the actual, concrete situation. It would be wrong, therefore, to say that the final lines, with their reference to miles of journey and sleep, make it "obvious" that the poem his some wider meaning. That obviousness is precisely what these lines are designed *not* to give. They only tease the reader. They alert him that the spell of the woods may be something that works elsewhere, but they say no more. They open a door, which his imagination is invited to pass through, but they themselves do not show him the way.

In having this suggestion of metaphor, "Stopping by Woods" is typical of a large number of Frost's poems. "The Cow in Apple Time," for instance, gives us directly only a description of the animal. She has tasted the sweetness of apples, and will no longer eat hay, though this leads to the painful shriveling of her udder. As the poem works upon the reader, however, there is the suggestion—though no more than a suggestion—that in this cow we also have a portrait of human experience, a fable of man's self-willed pursuit of sweetness. "Armful" describes a man who gradually loses control of the parcels piled up in his arms, and who finally drops them onto the road, in order to rearrange them into a better load. There are certain phrases in this account, however—"balanced at my breast," or trying to hold "with hand and mind/And heart"—that suggest a comparison between the man's experience with his parcels and his relation to the values and truths by which he lives. They, too, may be in such a disordered pile that they keep slipping out of his grasp. It may be well for him to set them down, too, and to look them over with a view to stacking them more carefully. Yet this comparison remains only a possibility, and there is nothing in the poem that makes it definite.

In "For Once, Then, Something" a man remarks how, when he looks down into a well, he usually sees the shiny surface picture of himself and the clouds over his head. Once, however, he thought he caught a glimpse of something "beyond the picture,/ Through the picture, a something white, uncertain,/ Something more of the depths." Does this poem simply describe a casual moment of rural experience for its own sake? Or is it a parable of man's search for underlying truth, which always hides from him behind the bright surface reflections of himself? Again, in "The Oven Bird" the song of this creature belongs to the midsummer world it inhabits, the world of hot dust and dead blossoms.

> The bird would cease and be as other birds
> But that he knows in singing not to sing.
> The question that he frames in all but words
> Is what to make of a diminished thing.

Does this question apply only to the bird? Or is it the question that hangs over the poet also, who must somehow sing in the midst of a dusty, blossomless, uninspiring world?

In all these poems, the concrete subject matter is just on the edge of turning into metaphor. But the poet holds back. He is controlled by some principle of restraint, some consideration that never allows him to turn away from the specific situation at hand. For the figure pausing by the woods, the "miles to go" and the "sleep" are what actually await him on this particular night. Everything said in "Armful," even the reference to mind and heart, bears directly on the struggle to balance parcels. The question about diminished things is posed by the oven bird, and by nothing else. The wider meanings are not brought into the foreground. They are never solidly nailed down in overt statement. They tease the reader, like something he glimpses out of the corner of his eye. The minute he tries to seize them and make them direct objects of his attention, they disappear.

III.

Another class of poems by Frost is represented by "Misgiving."

> All crying 'We will go with you, O Wind!'
> The foliage follow him, leaf and stem;
> But a sleep oppresses them as they go,
> And they end by bidding him stay with them.
>
> Since ever they flung abroad in spring
> The leaves had promised themselves this flight,
> Who now would fain seek sheltering wall,
> Or thicket, or hollow place for the night.
>
> And now they answer his summoning blast
> With an ever vaguer and vaguer stir,
> Or at utmost a little reluctant whirl
> That drops them no further than where they were.
>
> I only hope that when I am free
> As they are free to go in quest
> Of the knowledge beyond the bounds of life
> It may not seem better to me to rest.

In this poem Frost seems to have completely abandoned the technique of oblique suggestion. Far from keeping his attention fixed on the falling leaves, he ends with a statement of personal philosophy. Far from limiting his broader thrust to the insinuations of a word or two, he gives us a clear-cut analogy. As autumn leaves sink listlessly to earth beneath their own trees, so men at death may drift into rest, instead of leaping forward toward the new knowledge that awaits them. The poem does not hint at this comparison. It clearly states it.

However, if we look at Frost's lines, not in terms of the comparison made, but in terms of the metaphors realized, we discover a different situation. In the reading experience of this poem, the decisive point is not that a comparison is made, but that it has a dynamic quality. It does not rest at the level of simile, but moves on into the realm of metaphor. In the last stanza, to be sure, the fall of leaves and human death are presented side by side, and related in terms of one particular point of external resemblance. In the first three verses, however, in which the fall of leaves is described, we find that this situation is constantly threatening to turn into a human one. The leaves are "oppressed" by sleep; they "answer" the wind and "bid" it to stay; they "promise themselves" a flight; they "seek a sheltering wall." In each of the early stanzas, then, there are key words that portray the leaves' relation to the wind in human terms, and indicate that the leaves are an image of human life. There is a potential metaphor taking shape here. The natural situation is tending to change into a human situation. Therefore, even before the final stanza states the comparison in explicit terms, we are already aware of it in a metaphoric way. In fact, though the explicit comparison at the end adds clarity, it actually relates the two terms in a more static, more external, and therefore *less satisfying* way than the earlier stanzas do.

Once we point to the metaphoric dimension of the poem, we realize that here, too, Frost has been controlled by a principle of restraint. For the metaphoric tendency is nowhere carried through to completion. Though a metaphor is suggested again and again, no image appears to place it in clear focus. No decisive phrase enables us to see some aspect of a man in and through the concrete situation of the leaves. The two parts of the poem therefore beautifully complement each other. The first three stanzas have a metaphoric dynamism, but because the metaphor is not carried to completion, they need the clarity provided by the last stanza. That, in turn, states the point, but by means of such a static external comparison that it needs the earlier verses to give it some imaginative life. In any case, the poem is what it is because it *avoids metaphor*, because it is deliberately held back from completing its own poetic momentum. Frost apparently prefers a combination of incipient metaphor and flat comparison to the full intensity that a full metaphor can give. We can say that "Misgiving" is just as reserved as "Stopping by Woods on a Snowy Evening."

Frost has a number of poems in which he creates a metaphoric tendency but then lets it be turned aside into a stated comparison. In "The Onset" one stanza develops the analogy while the other works by suggestion. Frost is fully capable of writing a metaphor. Sometimes, as in "Devotion," he explicitly compares two things, but in such a way that they fuse together into a metaphoric unity.

> The heart can think of no devotion
> Greater than being shore to the ocean—
> Holding the curve of one position,
> Counting an endless repetition.

Even here, however, the explicit statement of the analogy has the effect on the imagination of separating the two items being compared. It inhibits the full realization of the metaphor. At the beginning the heart and the shore stand forth as parallel realities, each real in its own right, neither merely a metaphor for the other. The coalescing thrust of the last two lines never quite overcomes this initial separation. The same thing may be seen in "Birches," "A Patch of Old Snow," and "The Bear." However radically the two elements are brought together, the stated comparison is there, and reminds the imagination that each element is a separate and distinct thing.

I have concentrated here on the restraint Frost shows in

handling metaphors. He either suggests the metaphoric possibilities of his subject without letting them fully develop along his own lines, or he presents two things side by side in a straightforward comparison, so that the reader's imagination never enjoys the experience of watching one dissolve into the other. This same restraint, however, is to be found elsewhere in Frost. He often uses a colloquial style to keep in check whatever lyrical or imaginative impulses may arise, thus preventing them from ever taking complete control of his verse. He obstructs the driving thrust of some poetic insight by giving the lines a complicated sentence structure. In his dramatic narratives, he usually leaves the fundamental point of conflict between the characters unspoken. This is something indicated in the style and tone of the speaking voices, but it is not brought into clear focus through a decisive image or gesture.

What emerges at all these points is a determination by Frost *not* to make his own poetic lines appear adequate for his subject. His restraint conveys the impression that whatever his poem presents has a density and depth utterly beyond the neat competence of poetry. Both the poet and his reader must move respectfully around the outside of any object or situation, without obtruding into it.

IV.

What is the meaning of this peculiar poetic reserve? At one level we might say that it is an essential part of the speech that Frost has taken as his medium, the speech of rural New England. His poetic restraint reflects the reticence and habit of understatement in the Yankee manner. But this explanation is not sufficient. A poetic style does not function merely to reproduce the verbal peculiarities of some actual voices. Its validity lies in its power to recover the impact of immediate experience. We must therefore ask, What is Frost conveying through his poetic reserve? What aspect or quality in the immediate experience of the country world comes to expression here?

The poem "The Axe Helve" indicates the answer to these questions. A man tells us how the helve on his ax caused concern to Baptiste, a French-Canadian. The grain of the wood ran across it, instead of along its length. "Made on machine," Baptiste said, and with one good crack the head would have snapped right off. Baptiste then invited the other to his house, to show him his knowledge of helves and to give him one from his own supply.

> He showed me that the lines of a good helve
> Were native to the grain before the knife
> Expressed them, and its curves were no false curves
> Put on it from without. And there its strength lay
> For the hard work.

In this incident we see one fundamental quality in the country world where Frost moves. It is the knowledge of and respect for the particularity of each concrete thing. Men recognize that in all their dealings with the world they cannot simply impose their will from the outside. They must take into account the inherent quirks of each object, and must shape their own purposes accordingly. They must always follow the native grain. Imaginatively they do not see the world as made up of inert matter, which is simply waiting passively to be converted by bulldozer or factory into some new form. In the experience of country people, each particular place or object—each turn of the river, each season's rain, each ax handle—has an irreducible particularity of its own, a peculiar integrity that must be recognized and respected. If men are to fish that part of the river successfully, or to reap a harvest during that season, or to chop effectively with that ax handle, they must learn the quirks of whatever they deal with by a labor of patient familiarity. They certainly cannot assume that the world is standing ready to serve their purposes, or that they have sufficient power to force everything along their way. They do not share the urban man's belief in the machine, with its massive one-sided domination. They do not rely on a mass-produced but "irresistible" fishing lure, or on harvesting instructions issued by the government in Washington, or on a

standardized factory-made ax handle. They seek instead to become wise in the ways of each concrete place or thing, and to
attune their own efforts to it. They want to use the shapes that
already lie in the grain of the wood, and not to impose "false
curves" from without. They also believe that should a man forget to respect the particular items with which he must work,
should he begin to take them for granted or use them against
their nature, then he will immediately lose fruitful contact with
them. They will begin to obstruct and frustrate his efforts. They
will wither, instead of flourish, under his hands.[11] They will give
him no strength for the hard work. Yet even this frustration may
have beneficial results, by calling him back to his respect for the
concrete. In one poem Frost compares these helpful obstructions
to dust blown in the eyes [12] or to "A Tree Fallen Across the
Road."

> The tree the tempest with a crash of wood
> Throws down in front of us is not to bar
> Our passage to our journey's end for good,
> But just to ask us who we think we are
>
> Insisting always on our own way so.
> She likes to halt us in our runner tracks,
> And make us get down in a foot of snow
> Debating what to do without an axe.

In this rural outlook, the decisive fact about any situation is not
that it provides an occasion for new human projects, but that it
confronts all human projects with a tough density of its own.
This is the conviction behind so much of the down-to-earth practical realism in country attitudes.

At one level, Frost often contrasts this respect for the particular with other attitudes—especially with the single-minded func-
tionalism of the factory and the machine. But if he had only
presented it as part of his subject matter, as a quaint oddity in
the world out there, it would hardly merit our interest. The
poems would not make us experience it as a quality in the immediate feel of things. We would simply look at it from a dis-

tance, as we might look at strange animals in the zoo, and Frost would be just another purveyor of folk cuteness, like James Whitcomb Riley and Edgar Guest.

Frost, however, lets this respect for the particular control the language, and not just the subject matter, of his poetry. I am not referring simply to his preoccupation with individual concrete people and objects, the attentive way in which he notes them, describes them, and lets his lines rest in their presence. I also mean his almost instinctive care *never to let his own poetry obtrude upon them and overshadow them*. When some object appears in one of his poems, it does not dissolve in a metaphoric change. It does not lose its own distinctive identity, or disappear completely before another thing or a general idea. In poems such as "Stopping by Woods on a Snowy Evening" or "The Oven Bird," in which he works mainly by suggestion, he keeps his language faithfully focused on the actual scene or object. If there are wider meanings, he never allows them to step into the foreground and compete with what is concretely particular. The peace of the dark woods may be like death, and singing for diminished things may pose a task for poets, but to say as much would violate the most primitive discipline of the rural mind. Similarly, in a poem such as "Misgiving," he sets two things side by side in an explicit comparison. Yet in that way he preserves the concrete integrity of each. He does not let his poetic power dissolve either of them into a metaphor for the other.

In this way, Frost is able to convey to the listening ear a sense of the distinctive individuality that all things have in the thrust of concrete experience. They resist being absorbed into the will's projects or the mind's viewpoints or the imagination's metaphors, and even the most subtle impulses in the rhythm of speech must reflect the weight of their particularity.

In one sense, we can say that Frost's verse follows exactly the same direction as T. S. Eliot's earlier writing. It avoids every trace of maximal poetry. It rejects the language of exaltation. But in Frost this restraint has a totally different function. Instead of giving voice to the emotional emptiness of urban life, it serves to remind even city readers of a quality that still remains part of their concrete experience: the richness of each particular thing. Through Frost's style, respect for the concrete ceases to be simply an oddity of quaint New Englanders. It becomes an attitude imposed even upon the spontaneous impulses of the speaking voice. It is required and authenticated by the impact of immediacy.

For Frost, therefore, the snowy woods do not become an excuse for far-flung meditations, not simply because that is unlike the manner of country people, but because these woods in their concrete presence have an individual density of their own that cannot be ignored. *They* are what prevent even the poet's fancy from soaring wherever it will. This particular spot ("Between the woods and frozen lake") at this particular time ("The darkest evening of the year") in connection with these specific circumstances ("He gives his harness bells a shake")—claims from the spectator a steady attentiveness that is never relaxed. The poet can no more presume the adaptability of everything to his own purposes than can the farmer. He can no more impose the shapes of poetic discourse onto things from the outside than can the maker of ax helves. The native grain is what counts for everything—in objects, in places, and in people. Poetry works to bring out this native grain. It does not itself become the center of attention. It does not let the concrete become eclipsed by its own verbalizations.

We should take note of one point where Frost sometimes violates this principle of respect. Especially in his later work he shows a tendency to convert his poetry into teaching.

It is obviously proper and natural for a man to take the values that he finds in his experience and to convert them into a general philosophy. This is what Frost did with his respect for the concrete: he made it the basic principle in his personal view of things. For instance, he gave it a prominent place in his understanding of social matters. Individuals, he believed, should always keep a certain distance from each other and should not intrude into each other's lives. He criticized the modern school curriculum for what he called its "laid-on education," since it subjects all students to the same standardized program without reference to their individuality. He was vigorously opposed to all collectivistic movements. In 1931 he argued against the people who wanted all nations merged into a single world-wide government.

> I should want to say to anyone like that: Look! First I want to be a person. And I want you to be a person, and then we can be as interpersonal as you please. . . . But first of all you have got to have the personality. First of all, you have got to have the nations and then they can be as international as they please with each other.
> I should like to use another metaphor on them. I want my palette, if I am a painter, I want my palette on my thumb or on my chair, all clean, pure, separate colors. Then I will do the mixing on the canvas. The canvas is where the work of art is, where we make the conquest. But we want the nations all separate, pure, distinct, things as separate as we can make them; and then in our thoughts, in our arts, and so on, we can do what we please about it.[13]

His social views about persons and nations correspond perfectly to the status that individual things have in his own poetry—"all separate, pure, distinct, things as separate as we can make them."

There is nothing improper in the fact that Frost adopts this outlook. A poet has as much right as any other man to possess a general philosophy of his own. The trouble arises when Frost lets this viewpoint enter into his poetry in the form of abstract, authoritative generalities. Instead of keeping his language in disciplined response to the thrust of immediate experience and especially to the claims of the concrete particular, he lets it give voice to an idea that his mind has deliberately adopted. He uses his poetry to tell us what attitudes we should adopt to manage the world. As a poem develops, an insight or moral maxim will arise from the concrete situation, but will then break away with an independent life of its own. The voice of the teacher has suddenly replaced that of the poet.

We can see the problem here by comparing two of Frost's poems. In "The Exposed Nest" a principle for human conduct emerges, but in a very unobtrusive way. A girl and boy have come upon an exposed nest of baby birds. They consider building a protective screen to shield the birds, but then wonder whether the mother-bird might notice this and be frightened away permanently.

> We saw the risk we took in doing good,
> But dared not spare to do the best we could
> Though harm should come of it; so built the screen.

This "principle" never breaks free from the specific moment, as if it were an abstract truth perpetually valid in its own right. The ambiguous weight of this particular situation holds the center of the stage, and keeps the principle in a secondary place. In contrast, a poem such as "A Roadside Stand" proclaims the universal vice of do-gooding. It begins with a description of a specific stand, but this turns out to be merely the occasion for announcing a general moral principle that is true everywhere in its own right. Such a lapse as this, however, is an exception in Frost's work. It only serves to highlight his usual restraint and attentiveness before the concrete.

> Some may know what they seek in school and church,
> And why they seek it there; for what I search
> I must go measuring stone walls, perch on perch.[14]

V.

There is another aspect of Frost's restraint that we must now consider. In his world things not only have distinctive identities; they also have their own *capacity for communication*. Here we touch a point that sharply distinguishes rural and urban attitudes. In a metropolitan environment the individual finds that he must create many of his relations with the world largely by his own efforts. He has to find a job, acquire possessions, establish a name, make friends, and choose a church. And he has to do all this over again each time he moves. This is part of the mobility of modern life.

What is true of all these relations also applies to his role in communication. He does not see communication as a natural property of the world, as something that happens automatically between himself and his environment. Things do not take the initiative and spontaneously disclose themselves to him. As with other relationships, he believes that if any communication is to occur between him and the things or people around him, then he must create it by his own efforts. He therefore seeks a mutual understanding with another person chiefly by talking with him. He discovers the truth of the weather by reading man-made gauges and mastering man-made theories, by forcing upon it his own instruments of communication. People and things, he is taught, do not signify themselves. A man has to work on them with his concepts and language to catch a glimpse of their inner life. He must cover them with words in order to have them speak to him. Should he fail to do this, then they will always remain dumb. Ideas and words, in fact, are the only kind of communication in which the city has any confidence. It therefore fosters many thought and language industries.

This urban feeling that all human relationships with the world are man-made is not found in the country. There mobility does not dominate a person's existence. His relations with a certain place, a certain group of neighbors, a certain political party and church seem to be given to him with his birth. They are what reality imposes on him, not what he achieves by his own effort. His psychic energy is involved less in reaching out to achieve some contact with the world than in making the best of the contact that the world has already made with him.

In this perspective, communication is also felt to be a constituent in the structure of things. It is that which constantly happens *to men* rather than that which they produce. The assumption is that everything has its own way of betraying its inner secrets, and through long experience men have discovered these ways. Every rural area therefore has its own lore of signs that an individual must learn: how the leaves tell about tomorrow's weather, how buildings reveal the spirit of their inhabitants, how people convey their meaning by their tone of voice rather than by literal statement. In the country, far from trying to carry the whole burden of communication, human speech tends to play a secondary role. It follows after and takes note of the language of signs and hints. Compared to this natural kind of self-disclosure, this speech of things, the speech of words seems relatively flat and weak. In rural experience, much communication—and much of the best communication—between the world and man, and between man and man takes place without any use of words. This is something that people in the city find difficult to understand.

Confidence in the speech of things plays a role in Frost's poetry. The poet does not have to create all meanings himself, or to bestow a symbolic significance on things by means of his words. His primary task is to actualize the concrete reality of some object or situation, along with the hints that it itself gives of itself. He then relies on its power of communication to impress his reader. If his reader is incapable of responding to these hints and signs, if he is conscious of the meaning only of words and not of things, there is nothing the poet can do. This thing-language has its own character and its own richness, and no verbal equivalent can be substituted for it.

We can see this aspect of Frost's style in "Stopping by Woods on a Snowy Evening." He makes no effort there to provide us, directly or indirectly, with his own interpretation of the dark woods. It would be wrong to try to read this poem in terms of what Frost might have thought the woods to mean. The meaning lies not in what the poet makes of the concrete situation, but in what the concrete situation makes of itself through its own communicative power. The poet is not concerned to relate his readers, even secretly, to his own theory, but to put them in the presence of the actual scene, in such a way that they can feel *its* suggestive impact. Similarly, things in their concrete integrity have a way of echoing each other when they strike the responsive mind. The falling leaves resemble a listless old man. The shore that bears the pounding waves is like a faithful heart. These are not relations that men discover in things, but ones that are suggested by things. In his poems of explicit comparison, Frost lets the reader hear this echo in the things themselves. He does not make it seem to arise out of his own metaphoric power.

At the moments when Frost lapses into teaching, this quality in his verse is completely lost. Places and objects cease to speak with their own presence. We hear the poet announcing the truth of his own mind and standing forth alone in a silent universe as the only communicator. In these poems the world that is alive with natural communication has vanished. We are back in the city, listening to the endless monologues of self-conscious minds.

VI.

There is one more source of restraint in Frost's verse. It arises out of his conviction that in all genuine human relationships communication is achieved by *hints*. He once remarked, "With people you can trust you can talk in hints and suggestiveness. Families break up when people take hints you don't intend and miss hints you do intend." Hinting, in fact, is how people show trust for, and claim the unspoken understanding of, each other. In an early poem he observes that there is something barren in a relationship in which men have to "speak the literal to inspire/ The understanding of a friend." [15] When a person acts in this way, it means that he does not think that others will reach toward him with their perception and imagination. He believes that they are only static and indifferent toward him, and can be made aware of his meaning only when he blatantly explains himself to them. However, a human relationship is equally barren when a man does not let others use their initiative and imagination in response to him. He insists on his own activity dominating the situation. He wants them to be passively receptive in his presence, to think nothing except what he has literally and elaborately spelled out for them.

In Frost's perspective hinting is the one kind of language that fully respects the other person. It invites him to make an effort to understand. It respects the distance between people, and does not imagine that this distance can be closed by the efforts of one party alone, however expert his techniques may be. It accepts the fact that in every human relationship a man should want to go only halfway, out of respect and desire for the free movement of the other toward him. In Frost's view, any time someone refuses that distance to others and begins to imagine that his own activity is quite sufficient to make contact with them, then he has become immoral. However well intentioned he may be, he has in effect denied them the right to make their own free response. He does not wait for them to advance toward him with sensitivity and attention. He refuses to meet them at the always uncertain but genuinely human level of mutual give-and-take. He thinks of his relationship with them simply as the product of his own activity. He therefore violates their integrity.

This respect for the free response of other persons is a recurrent theme in Frost's work. He finds it lacking in the recent preoccupation of middle-class Americans to help the poor. Their sympathy, he believes, does not recognize a capacity for response in those who suffer. It is absorbed in a purely one-sided effort to do good. It does not dignify the poor, but simply manipulates them with kindness. Indeed, any feeling of charity that is not restrained by a respect for the self-initiated action of others is essentially corrupt.

For Frost, this same moral requirement applies to the whole event of communication. A speaker must always so fashion his statements that he gives room to the perceptiveness and imagination of those who hear him. He must not say too much. The teacher who explains everything, or the lover who puts all his feelings into words, is depriving others of an active role and is unwittingly degrading them. Everyone who speaks must recognize the distance—the "abyss"—that lies between himself and other men.

> Far as we aim our signs to reach,
> Far as we often make them reach,
> Across the soul-from-soul abyss,

> There is an aeon-limit set
> Beyond which they are doomed to miss.[16]

The speaker must want and affirm this distance in the style of all his statements. In other words, he must at times be content with hints, and not try to make up for a possible lack of response in others by smothering them with clear-cut statements. He must invite their sympathetic initiative. He must let them know that this distance can and should be crossed only when they, for reasons wholly their own and forever inaccessible to him, let their minds reach toward him. He must be as respectful of their integrity in his speaking as he is of the integrity of places and tools in his work.

Here is a third source of Frost's poetic reserve. He indicates metaphoric possibilities, but he deliberately leaves room for the imagination of his readers. His meanings and images have the status of hints, rather than lessons. He wants his own capacities as a poet to fire up, but not to displace, the poetic vivacity in his audience.

VII.

Members of the Christian community are always being tempted by a false spirituality. In their relationship with God they often seek grounds for turning from the needs and confusions of concrete immediacy. They hope to enjoy a clean, untroubled air in their religion. They keep forgetting that as long as they are in the flesh, their Christian life is a way and not an end; that it takes them beyond the world only by directing them into the world, beyond themselves by confronting them with themselves, and beyond death by leading them into death.

We examined one kind of evasion in connection with Eliot's verse: the failure of the Christian community to realize its involvement with the changing conditions of immediacy. It does not always keep itself engaged in the concrete. It remains insensitive to the new kinds of vitality that give form to daily experience. It ignores the new modes of suffering that are constantly gathered into a man's life with God.

In our day, this failure has been most conspicuous in terms of the modern, industrial, overcrowded city. The Christian community has been reluctant to absorb the images, the rhythms, and the despairs of this human sphere. It has preferred to help men escape from this city-world, trying to give them an inspirational attitude toward their dreary work, trying to foster a cult of personal love between each of them and their four million immediate neighbors, trying to encourage individualized morality in a society of mass movements. It has failed to accept the feel and taste of urban existence, and to be confident in the sufficiency of God's grace even there. It has given the completely false impression that Christians cannot thrive in the midst of loneliness or violence or emotional emptiness, that they must operate only within a cosy, intimate situation of person-to-person fellowship.

Whenever Christian churches become caught up in this kind of evasion, they betray themselves in their language. Their sermons and prayers have a way of creating an atmosphere far removed from the daily life. In its phrasing and rhythms their speech seems to belong to some bygone or artificial world. That is why poets like Eliot, who explore the new sound-values in everyday speech and who thereby bring the new conditions of immediacy into focus, are always of indispensable service to the Christian community.

The importance of this problem, however, must not be taken to mean that Christian discourse has no other task but that of keeping up-to-date, that it should commit itself unreservedly to prevailing habits of speech. The first allegiance of Christians is to their Lord. Because their Lord has created and sustained the actual world, has Himself entered into it and made it His own, and has made them His instruments for its complete redemption, this actual world must be included in their allegiance to Him. But what is this actual world of their fleshly existence? Is it that disclosed by the current habits of daily speech? In part, yes. But *only in part*. For while daily speech is particularly responsive to certain aspects of immediacy, it is also negligent of others. Like every act of the human consciousness, it is selective. In providing a rich perception of some of the things that engage human life at any moment, it persistently avoids others.

This means that the language of the Christian community cannot simply absorb the prevailing habits of speech. In certain respects, it must also surpass and even counteract them; that is, insofar as they obscure the concrete life of flesh. It must not be simply up-to-date. It must be catholic, in the traditional meaning of that term, representing within itself, as the subject of God's life-giving grace, every variety of immediate human perception. It must therefore speak always in a variety of living styles. While not turning its back on new patterns of idiom and rhythm, neither must it limit itself to these.

Frost's verse points up one aspect of immediacy that urban speech and urban experience persistently disregard: the stubborn integrity of each particular thing. Of course, there is a basis for this evasion. The city does flood the human consciousness with such an indigestible mass of objects that no single item can make much of an impact or establish the reality of its own peculiar being. Each entity exists only as an instance of a class—delinquent, Chevrolet, Negro, fountain pen. Assaulted by this endless sea of objects, a man uses all his mental effort just to sort out the general types of things that loom before him in each moment of awareness. He is absorbed in preparing some clumsy kind of response before the next wave of objects comes along. He does not have the country man's time to savor the particularity of this or that specific detail.

At the same time, the city is built and sustained by man's purposeful violation of individual things. It is a world which he has created, and within which nothing is allowed to have any integrity but his own self-willed "projects." People there are identified exhaustively with their jobs. Beyond the functions that they perform as workers, parents, voters, or soldiers, they have no further reality, no private identities incommunicably their own. They are the enterprises that they serve. Nature in turn is considered to be only a reservoir of "raw" materials, waiting for

the bulldozer or the factory to absorb it in some human project
and thus give it a meaning.

In spite of all these circumstances, however, the claim of
particularity still makes itself felt in city experience. Think of all
those, for instance, who develop a feel for the concrete individuality of their automobiles. They learn their weaknesses and idiosyncracies, how best to accelerate them, how best to brake them.
Like Frost's maker of ax helves, they instinctively try to follow
the native grain of their machines when they drive them. Or
think of the high value given to family relationships, in which
even city people are confronted by the dense and unmanageable
complexity of the individual. While urban speech habits take
little cognizance of this feeling for particularity, it continues to
operate below the surface, and makes Frost's verse seem valid
even for the city reader.

The Christian community finds itself bound to respect the
particularity of things—that is, not only to have that respect as a
self-conscious pose, but to reflect it spontaneously in its very
manner of speaking. For if the incarnate existence of Jesus Christ
means that God gathers men into His eternal life, it also means
that He establishes his own Lordship over them and their world.
It deprives them of any license to use everything for their own
purposes, and to dismiss the reality of anything or anyone insofar
as it is not absorbed into their projects. God himself is the Crea-
tor of all things. He establishes them in their indissoluble dis-
tinctness, and proclaims that each creature respect the integrity
of all others.

The Christian life therefore does not put an individual person
in proud superiority over his natural or social environment. Human words are not the only medium for God's self-communica-
tion. He has ordained that men listen, not only to themselves,
but also to the language of concrete things—the baptismal water,
the sacramental bread and wine. He awakens men to love each
other, but not to do so with a one-sided sympathy that wants
only to take away pain, or with a self-expansive friendliness that
knows no reserve. Christian love involves a mutual withdrawal,
in which each person allows others the dignity to be what they

are under God. "Who are you," Paul asks, "to pass judgment on the servant of another? It is before his own master that he stands or falls. And he will be upheld, for the Master is able to make him stand." (Rom. 14:4.) The effect of divine grace is always to increase, rather than minimize, a man's sense of the distance that separates him from the other creatures around him. They belong to his God and not to him, and have a holy integrity that he cannot abuse. He is called to serve them, but only modestly and with hesitation, never forgetting both his own feebleness and God's sufficiency for them.

If we consider the Christian community today, we find it remarkably indifferent to this kind of reserve. It lets itself be too fully caught up in its own God-given tasks. It forgets that all creatures, and not just committed Christians, are the servants of God and agents of His will, whether they wish to be or not. It does not preserve an attitude of respect before the otherness of things. It is too dazzled by the overriding importance of its own religious projects. Its concern to bring about salvation, or to relieve suffering, or to avoid sin threatens to crowd away its recognition of the rest of reality. It is plagued by a presumptuous activism, by a compulsion to challenge, rebuke, or improve every situation. A man's freedom in Christ to accept himself and to accept all other things is in constant danger of neglect. In this regard, Christians today are influenced too much, rather than too little, by their urban environment. They can hardly understand Milton's insight that "they also serve who only stand and wait."

This lack of respect and restraint before a concrete world, this compulsion to see every situation only as an occasion for performing service, certainly shows itself in the working language of Christian groups. We rarely hear a preaching style of understatement, in which decisive points are not encapsulated in smooth phrases, and in which the events and signs of the Bible are allowed to convey their own rich meaning, without being reduced to some verbal generality. Sermons have a compulsion to spell everything out. Why is there not more suspicion of human words? They may be an ordained medium for divine action, but they are not the only medium. Man's whole existence is drenched in God's communicative power. The domination of speech may reflect a suspicion that God cannot be trusted and that only man-made communications, like man-made environments, are reliable.

In this context, Frost's verse is a healthy influence. He celebrates the particularity of things. He lets them stand in their own right, without making them seem like instruments of his own meaning. Few Christians know anything firsthand about the particular New England scene that he explores, but they certainly have reasons to share in his kind of relation toward the world.

Of course, that respect for particular things does not come easily to men. It involves humility, and humility is a costly virtue. For a city man to recognize the stubborn particularity of individual things involves a shocking rupture between himself and the world around him, an undercutting of his preoccupation with his own projects—including his "Christian" projects—and with people and things as his instruments. It means the frustration of one of the most basic forms of human pride, the pride of dominating action, the precise kind of pride that thrives in the city.

Such humility is not something that Christians produce within themselves. It flows from the knowledge God gives them of his glory and of his Lordship over all the concrete world. That Lordship means that things have their existence primarily in relation to Him, and therefore stand over against men with their own integrity. Because of that Lordship, no person can expect them to speak to him whenever he wishes, or to yield to him whatever he desires. And if they speak, it will be in their own way. They are not his creatures, nor does he depend essentially on them. His life is with his Lord. Therefore he can face and accept the distance between himself and the world around him, the abyss that separates him from his neighbors. He can let things be what they are, even in the moments when they confront him with a terrifying blankness and break his work to pieces, when they mock his charitable projects. He can be instructed by Frost's diction. He can also share in that tough-mindedness which is required in all genuine respect for the concrete. Because he really allows the concrete to have its own integrity, he stands ready and willing for it to be its unmanageable self, even at the expense of his Christian aspirations. As Frost reminds him,

> Be glad of water, but don't forget
> The lurking frost in the earth beneath
> That will steal forth after the sun is set
> And show on the water its crystal teeth.[17]

NOTES FOR CHAPTER THREE

1. Quotations from Robert Frost's poetry are all taken from *Complete Poems of Robert Frost* (New York: Holt, Rinehart and Winston, Inc., 1949). By permission of the publishers.

2. See E. R. Curtius, *European Literature and the Latin Middle Ages,* trans. Willard Trask (New York: Pantheon Books, Inc., 1953), pp. 187–200.

3. Vergil *Georgics* II. 467.

4. Frost, *op. cit.,* p. 81.

5. *Ibid.,* p. 177.

6. See *ibid.,* p. 88.

7. See *ibid.,* p. 118.

8. See *ibid.,* p. 314.

9. See *ibid.,* p. 396.

10. See *ibid.,* p. 386.

11. See *ibid.,* p. 401.

12. See *ibid.,* p. 341.

13. Robert Frost, "Education by Poetry," *The Amherst Graduates' Quarterly,* XX, pp. 84f.

14. ———, *Complete Poems . . . ,* p. 214.

15. *Ibid.,* p. 27.

16. *Ibid.,* p. 436.

17. *Ibid.,* p. 358.

Chapter Four

Artificial Speech: *Wallace Stevens*

IN THE CASE OF Eliot and of Frost, we have poets who move within the realm of ordinary speech. They use a vocabulary and a syntax that might actually be heard on the street or on the farm. They do not simply reproduce this language, of course. By controlling its rhythm and images, they give it an unusual intensity and realize its latent capacity for the concrete. Nevertheless, their poems sound as if they were spoken by a normal person. As Eliot says, they mean to give their readers the satisfaction of saying, "That is how I should talk if I could talk poetry." These poets accept the risk of being prosaic, in the interests of doing what they can with the common style.

In every age, this is the most prevalent kind of poetry. But alongside of it there occasionally appears an *eccentric* poetry. The aim here is not to explore what can be done within the patterns of ordinary speech, but to develop an artificial language, and to do so for the sake of catching aspects of immediate experience suppressed by ordinary speech. An eccentric style is a much more difficult achievement than one might think. The habits of daily conversation are deeply sunk within the consciousness of every man, and it is extremely hard to break free from them. Greater still is the risk of self-exhibitionism. The poet who writes in a peculiar style of his own can easily forget his allegiance to the concrete. He can become preoccupied with his own originality and with the impression of oddity that he makes on others. Or he can become resentful that he is not better understood.

The development of an eccentric poetry involves so many hazards and requires such sustained self-discipline that there are few writers who have been successful with it. One thinks of Gerard Manley Hopkins and William Blake. The outstanding example in English is probably John Milton. His style is as far removed as possible from common speech. He has invented a kind of personal language of his own. But he never loses touch with the perceptual world. He has seized and explored dimensions of immediate experience that are too exceptional for everyday speech, too majestic and capacious. He has caught an imaginative dazzle in the impact of things that requires an eccentric style. What validates his work is his constant fidelity to concrete perception.

In recent years, one poet in America has successfully developed an eccentric style. He is Wallace Stevens (1879–1955).[1] Stevens has the most thoroughly "modern" outlook of the poets studied in this volume. He was enthusiastic about the works of the *avant garde* in painting, sculpture, and music. Indeed the great turning point in his own poetic development took place after he was deeply affected by an exhibition of modern art in Hartford, Connecticut, in 1934.

This modernity is striking if we remember that Stevens was not one of the disillusioned expatriates who fled to Paris after the First World War. He was born in the eighteen-seventies, along with Amy Lowell and Vachel Lindsay and Frost and Sandburg. He studied law, became a member of the bar in 1904, practiced in New York until 1916, when he joined the Hartford Accident and Indemnity Company as head of its Surety Claims Department. By the time the young expatriates were cavorting around Europe, Stevens was a middle-aged businessman, commuting to the office each morning and gradually rising up the executive ladder. In 1934 he became vice-president of his company, and later, in addition, vice-president of the Hartford Livestock Insurance Company.

This is the man who developed and successfully controlled an eccentric style of poetry. In his verse he has no concern with exploring the possibilities of ordinary speech. He wants to actualize an aspect of immediate experience that ordinary speech

ignores. He focuses on what might be called the impact of nature
—not the dead, objectified nature of rational science, but those
moments when the mind is seized by the elemental impressions
of light and air and has not begun to identify any "objects." To
catch this order of experience, to explore the world that a man
sees when he forgets his social role-playing self and is caught up
by the weather and the sun, "To expugn all people and be a
pupil/Of the gorgeous wheel" [2]—this is the aim of Stevens' curious style. So successful are his poems that they pose a serious
challenge to the common-sense view of things. They also raise a
fundamental question about the Christian habit of portraying
God's creation as a universe of fixed entities.

I.

Stevens' verse shares the mark of all eccentric poetry. It is very
difficult to understand. Stevens has often been called "a poet's
poet." That is, his verse poses so many problems for the reader
that only an insider—a person who actually writes poetry himself
—can understand it.

Consider, for example, the following poem of eighteen lines.

Unsnack your snood, madanna, for the stars
Are shining on all the brows of Neversink.

Already the green bird of summer has flown
Away. The night-flies acknowledge these planets,

Predestined to this night, this noise and the place
Of summer. Tomorrow will look like today,

Will appear like it. But it will be an appearance,
A shape left behind, with like wings spreading out,

Brightly empowered with like colors, swarmingly,
But not quite molten, not quite the fluid thing,

A little changed by tips of artifice, changed
By the glints of sound from the grass. These are not

> The early constellations, from which came the first
> Illustrious intimations—uncertain love,
>
> The knowledge of being, sense without sense of time.
> Take the diamonds from your hair and lay them down.
>
> The deer-grass is thin. The timothy is brown.
> The shadow of an external world comes near.[3]

What possibly can be made of this?

The first few lines set the time as a summer night, but do so in a puzzling way. Why is there such a whimsical opening? What are "the brows of Neversink"? Granted that the green bird has flown away, what does that have to do with night-flies? Why do night-flies "acknowledge" these planets? Why is it relevant that these planets are "predestined" to this night and this noise? And what is this "noise," anyway? Why is the day compared to a bird? What are the "early constellations," and why should they be a source of profound experiences? Before any of this can be explained, however, the "madanna" of the opening line is addressed again, though instead of unsnacking her snood she is now told to take the diamonds from her hair. Diamonds? What diamonds?

The reader will probably not bother to ask. For at last he comes upon a clear and straightforward line: "The deer grass is thin. The timothy is brown." The dizzying flow of elusive statements has finally been stopped. The blur of obscure associations has dissolved into a familiar, objective, and non-disintegrating scene. If this is what happens to the poet's language when "the shadow of the external world comes near," the reader might wish that Stevens had stayed in that shadow more often.

There is still one last hope. Some authors, when they write an obscure poem, try to provide a helpful key in their title. Unfortunately, Stevens is not one of these. He calls this piece "Late Hymn from the Myrrh-Mountain."

Fortunately the difficulty here cannot be removed by an interpreter. There is no viewpoint we can adopt that will make everything simple and obvious. There is no key to turn the obscurities into familiar, commonplace truths. I say this is fortunate, because if understanding the poetry means getting rid of the difficulty, then the difficulty has no business being there in the first place. It would be a veneer arbitrarily imposed by the poet—not a means for elucidating reality or enhancing the reader's consciousness, but an irrelevant obstruction, a verbal game of wits between author and reader.

Stevens' poems are almost all difficult because they speak out of a very peculiar relation to reality. They are intended to confront the reader with a very unusual awareness of the world and to prevent him from retreating into any of his conventional attitudes. The difficulty, then, is not in the order of language but in the order of experience and perception. It belongs to the substance of Stevens' work, and not just to the manner of its execution.

For purposes of discussion, let me examine in sequence two quite different strands of difficulty that are bound to frustrate any new reader of Stevens—the problem of becoming interested in the poems, and the problem of understanding them.

II.

Of these two, the problem of interest is the more fundamental. In general, once a poem intrigues us, we become positively motivated to absorb its style. We willingly let our awareness be guided sensitively by the pull and tug of its verbal novelties. When a poem fails to intrigue us, however, every obscurity in its style becomes another source of exasperation. It seems to prove that the author is deliberately trying to trick his reader.

In the case of Stevens, we cannot glance at three pages of his verse without wondering why he has bothered to write. If, for instance, we work on "Late Hymn," and do penetrate through the obscurity of green birds, molten days, and brown timothy, what else have we gained but a momentary impression of how summer passes away? And who wants to wrestle through verbal obscurities for that meager benefit?

Whatever else a poem may do, it must present a situation electric with significant change. It must hold the reader's interest, not simply by having certain unusual things happen to its subject, but by creating an atmosphere in which *anything* can happen, full of possible surprises and unexpected disclosures. When this is done, every element in the scene becomes fraught with interest. Even the slightest change may be the beginning of a dramatic upheaval. The reader grows alert to the slightest tremor, and is therefore glad for the ebb and flow of the rhythm to help guide his attentiveness. If a poet fails on this point, and leaves us wondering why anyone should take the trouble to write —or even read—his lines, then all his artistry might as well be tossed away.

Consider how Tennyson begins a section of his poem "Maud" (1855).

> Dead, long dead,
> Long dead!
> And my heart is a handful of dust,
> And the wheels go over my head,
> And my bones are shaken with pain,
> For into a shallow grave they are thrust,
> Only a yard beneath the street,
> And the hoofs of the horses beat, beat . . .

A voice from the dead, a voice speaking with this ominous pulsating rhythm, a voice located not in heaven but in a disintegrated body just under the surface of some busy, bustling, life-filled thoroughfare—what could be more intriguing? We do not know what will develop, but we have been grasped by a situation that seems full of surprises. Again, consider the opening lines of Robert Browning's ballad "How They Brought the Good News from Ghent to Aix" (1845).

> I sprang to the stirrup, and Joris, and he;
> I galloped, Dirck galloped, we galloped all three;
> "Good speed!" cried the watch, as the
>   gatebolts undrew;

"Speed!" echoed the wall to us galloping
   through . . .

We are thrust immediately into the middle of things, without explanation, and join the situation just as it explodes into action. Even if we have no idea where Ghent is, or Aix, and have never heard of the wars of the Dutch against the Spanish, the situation has a quality of commanding drama that confers importance on every detail.

In contrast to these two examples, one well may wonder how many people would have their attention aroused by the atmosphere of Pope's "Essay on Criticism" (1711).

'Tis hard to say, if the greater want of skill
Appear in writing or in judging ill;
But, of the two, less dang'rous is th' offence
To tire our patience, than mislead our sense.

.   .   .   .

Learn then what morals Critics ought to show,
For 'tis but half a Judge's task, to know.
'Tis not enough, taste, judgment, learning join;
In all you speak, let truth and candour shine.

A reader would have little trouble with Pope's language. The ideas are lucid and shrewd; the wit is bright and sometimes funny. The real difficulty would arise from the lack of significance in the total situation. In real life, the world of literary judgment may very well be vibrant with spite and wisdom, with passionate convictions and human conflict. But in the experience of most people, this is a very trivial world, and has the effect of trivializing whatever occurs within it. For this reason, Pope's great truths may sound rather flat and his earnestness seem almost ridiculous.

Such qualities, of course, do not characterize Pope's "Essay" only. What of those interminable sonnet sequences of the sixteenth century, in which romantic love is set in the midst of

Cupid's arrows, pale moonlight, and posturing despair? What of those tiresome descriptions of English rural life in the eighteenth century, which always present the "village green" and always dwell on the peace at "eventide"? What of the moral exhortations that must have appealed to our great-grandfathers, in which Truth sat shining on some mountaintop and the struggle with oneself for purity gave life its excitement? Could we expect any startling surprises from the mechanical optimism of Tennyson's "Will" (1855)?

> O well for him whose will is strong!
> He suffers, but he will not suffer long;
> He suffers, but he cannot suffer wrong:
> For him nor moves the loud world's random mock,
> Nor all Calamity's hugest waves confound.

These are probably all "difficult" poems to read, not difficult to understand but difficult to become interested in. The situation that activates them and gives them an atmosphere of possibility and surprise no longer seems important.

Now this is precisely the kind of difficulty that will bedevil every new reader of Wallace Stevens. We can certainly be made attentive by a voice from the dead, or by galloping horses bursting forth into the night, or even by "the smells of steaks in passageways," since recent poetry has made us aware of the surprising shocks and incongruities that may leap at us in the city. But who can be aroused by the way summer begins to disappear, as in "Late Hymn from the Myrrh-Mountain"? What significant surprises could possibly be effected by the change from one season to another, or from one part of the day to another? Who is concerned with a fanciful description of the dawn,[4] or with a meditation on blossoming dogwood trees,[5] or with a celebration of the evening star?[6] What is the point of portraying "The Green Plant" or "The Yellow Afternoon," "The Women in Sunshine" or "The Bouquet of Roses in Sunlight," the "Variations on a Summer Day" or "The Auroras of Autumn"? Stevens has a poem about February, which begins:

The brooks are bristling in the field,
Now, brooks are bristling in the fields
And gelid Januar has gone to hell.

The water puddles puddles are
And ice is still in Februar.
It still is ice in Februar.[7]

Who cares? Can this world of changing sunlight and weather
ever be significant enough, ever be dynamic or explosive enough
to win our alertness and justify our concentration?

The obstacle here is enormous, and can be summed up in one
phrase: the modern attitude toward nature.

On the one hand, most people today are so far removed from
the elements of sun and weather, so deeply engulfed in that endless tissue of human purposes, human institutions, and human
obligations that make up the city that for them nature has no
personal meaning whatsoever. They never see the sky, except
on a technicolor movie screen. The stars are wholly invisible in
the constant blaze of house lights and city lights. The only emotions that they publicly express about the weather are disgust at
the fuel bills it brings in winter, and annoyance at the humidity
it brings in summer. Nature is too far removed from them to be
a region of ominous and significant change.

On the other hand, men today carry in their minds a picture
or understanding of nature that reinforces this psychic withdrawal. This is derived from the physics of the seventeenth century, and may be sketched in three points.

1. It is an accepted axiom that the immediate and instan-
taneous appearance of nature to our senses is completely untrust-
worthy. The Copernican theory provides the classic and decisive case. As far as our "unaided" eye can tell, the sun seems
to move, rising at dawn and setting at dusk. The very persistence
of these phrases in our language shows how compelling this
appearance is. Yet we believe that in fact no such thing happens, that the sun stays still, and that we on earth are the ones
turned round and round. This suspicion of appearances is ex-

tended to the whole domain of nature. The butterfly is not understood by an eye that has been captivated by its color, but by impeccable photographs, laboratory dissections, and experimental mutations. The substance of a stone is not understood by the hand, for in spite of its seeming hardness it is thought to be actually a porous constellation of molecular bonds. No one today could possibly credit the "unaided" senses. We have been schooled to believe that when nature imposes itself upon our naked flesh, without the help of some scientific instrument, we are then not in contact with it as it truly is. We are being deceived by mere "appearances."

2. As the complement of this first point, men have long believed that nature is accessible in its true character only through precise measurements. Or rather, in John Locke's famous formulation, only the measurable aspects of a natural object—its solidity, its size, its shape, and its movements—really belong to it. The rest, such as its colors, sounds, tastes, etc., are what John Locke calls its secondary qualities—that is, they are nothing in the object itself but are sensations produced by the object *in us*.[8] In other words, nature is actually a mass of blank, colorless, odorless *matter*, known not by the stimulated senses, but only by the abstract measurements of the rational mind. "Matter," it should be remembered, does not represent anything that we experience, but designates what is left in an object after all its sensuous (or secondary) qualities have been taken away. This abstract notion of "matter," then, perfectly expresses the modern way of picturing nature.

When this materialistic view first began to attract attention at the turn of the eighteenth century, it dismayed and depressed most people. It meant that nature could never again be naively enjoyed. It could never be a home, but only an "environment."

Our souls [Joseph Addison wrote in 1711] are at present delightfully lost and bewildered in a pleasant delusion, and we walk about like the enchanted hero of a romance, who sees beautiful castles, woods, and meadows; and at the same time hears the warbling of birds and the purling of streams;

but upon the finishing of some secret spell, the fantastic
scene breaks up, and the disconsolate knight finds himself
on a barren heath or in a solitary desert.[9]

This, however, was over two hundred years ago. The children of
today show little sense of loss for the warbling birds and purling
streams. They accept the barren heath which they think surrounds them, the world of blank matter and energy.

3. Mention must be made, finally, of the scientific emphasis
on repetition in the behavior of nature. This has created in most
minds the picture of nature as a realm of fixed regularity. In contrast to the human scene, where freedom and passion constantly
produce unexpected reversals, nature is subject to rigid law and
its events are essentially predictable. Surprises are out of the
question. What has happened yesterday will happen today and
tomorrow—the sun, the rain, the cold, the heat—and if there
are important changes, they will occur too slowly and too gradually to be seen.

This general outlook toward nature belongs to the unthink-
ingly and culturally determined side of people's minds. It must
not be confused with science itself. We should also note that
events today are conspiring to erode this picture of things. The
idea of nuclear energy has begun to work upon the public mind.
Matter is beginning to be viewed as packets of violence, rather
than as inert stuff, and nature is seen more as a series of explo-
sions than as a smoothly running machine. Nevertheless, the
materialistic outlook still prevails in the habits of ordinary life,
and still leads people to believe that there is nothing significant
in *their own* direct experience of the physical world.

It is this outlook that finds Stevens' poetry trivial and therefore difficult. Change in his world usually arises out of the sunlight and the weather, as when the green sea becomes a glisten-
ing blue, or when "the green bird of summer has flown away."

Stevens takes this as his focus because he finds nothing trivial
here. He repudiates the abstract and rational approach to nature.
For him, the envelope of air and light that surrounds us is primarily something immediately experienced, not something arti-

ficially fabricated by measurements, diagrams, and equations. Stevens seeks to portray this envelope as it appears to immediate experience, and what he finds is far from a realm of routine mechanism. Everyone knows in what deep and subtle ways the sunlight and the seasons can affect the human spirit. A man may think of himself as caught up wholly in the human world of tasks and institutions, and he may imagine that he notices the weather only to make conversation. In actual fact he lives *in it* with a good deal more psychic involvement than he realizes. Such things as rain or sun, cold or heat, a bright spring morning or a dreary autumn afternoon can have a profound influence upon his emotional buoyancy. At a particular moment they may make all the difference as to how effectively he works at his job or participates in some social affair. This weather experience is the domain of Stevens' poetry. He explores what touches the consciousness here and what is able to affect it so deeply. This is something more than blank matter or dull regularity, something of overwhelming significance, whose slightest change can put a man's mind on edge.

Such a radical perspective cannot possibly be reconciled with the conventional and largely man-centered sources of interest that nourish most literature. To find Stevens interesting means to let go of some deep-set habits of mind, and to be led to a new experience of nature—something no one can go through without an immense mental effort. Anyone who neglects that effort will retain the conventional outlook upon nature, and will find Stevens a very trivial poet. Yet this is the task that Stevens pursues. On every page of his work he seeks to win his readers on this fundamental point, to get them to recognize as their own a nature that has nothing to do with blank matter or dull regularity, that is not "nature" at all, in the sense of being a neutral realm out there. He wants them to feel the impact of the weather in a new way,

> to catch from that
>
> Irrational moment its unreasoning,
> As when the sun comes rising, when the sea

Clears deeply, when the moon hangs
　　on the wall

Of heaven-haven. These are not things
　　transformed.
Yet we are shaken by them as if
　　they were.
We reason about them with a later reason.[10]

Like the early Eliot, Stevens seeks to bring language to a dimension of fleshly experience that has become inarticulate. In contrast to Eliot, however, he does not take us into the din of the city, but into the impact of air, sun, and weather. This is the road he follows to the end, and follows with such extraordinary skill that he must be ranked with Eliot in poetic achievement.

III.

We now turn from the difficulty of interest to the other difficulty that confronts us in Stevens' work, the problem of his obscure style. Here also we must refer to certain habitual attitudes regarding nature that generally prevail. This time, however, the attitudes do not bear upon what nature is, but how it is to be presented for man's enjoyment.

People today do find enjoyment in the "beauties" of nature. How many families eat breakfast beside a calendar picture of the majestic Alps or the warm English countryside! *The National Geographic Magazine* provides a monthly package of glossy scenes. The vacation trip to the woods or beach brings the climactic moment in the yearly rhythm of family life. And who can minimize the service of poetry to this enjoyment? For centuries it has resisted the mechanical view of nature and the urbanizing degradation of life. As was pointed out in an earlier chapter, poetry long ago became identified with the pleasure of escaping from the city and relishing those very bird songs and purling streams that Addison thought had been completely dispelled by the new scientific philosophy.

> I will arise and go now, and go to Innisfree,
> And a small cabin build there, of clay and wattles
> made:
> Nine bean rows will I have there, a hive for the
> honey bee,
> And live alone in the bee-loud glade.
>
> .   .   .   .
>
> I will arise and go now, for always night and day
> I hear lake water lapping with low sounds by the
> shore;
> While I stand on the roadway, or on the pavements
> gray,
> I hear it in the deep heart's core.

W. B. Yeats, "The Lake Isle of Innisfree" (1893).

If we examine the "nature" that is enjoyed here, however, we
find that it is no more full of surprises than is the nature studied
by science. The scenes on the calendar or in *The National Geographic* do not fascinate us, for they do not catch moments of
vital change. The lake isle of Innisfree, the meadows, the flowers,
and all the other "beauties" presented by this kind of poetry do
not compel our attention, because they do not present an electric atmosphere in which life and truth hang in the balance. On
the contrary, *nothing* significant happens, and *that is precisely
the enjoyable quality* in this presentation of nature. "Good-bye,
proud world! I'm going home," Emerson wrote (1847).

> I am going to my own hearth-stone,
> Bosomed in yon green hills alone,—
> A secret nook in a pleasant land,
> Whose groves the frolic fairies planned;
> Where arches green, the live-long day,
> Echo the blackbird's roundelay,
> And vulgar feet have never trod
> A spot that is sacred to thought and God.

Nature in this context is designed to take us away from the
shock and surprise of real life, away from the reality that con-

stantly intrudes upon us and frustrates our desires. It is designed to provide a fantasy land of wish-fulfillment, a realm planned by "frolic fairies," where the dynamic and unpredictable world has completely vanished, and where we are able to enjoy a state of dreamlike pleasure.

The decisive feature in this presentation of nature is that the ingredients are arranged to form a *self-contained scene*. Whether verse or camera is the medium, the aim is always to create the illusion of a static, three-dimensional space, where nature is beautiful and the current of human wishing can flow untroubled. Above are the blue sky and floating clouds. Beneath are the dark, moist earth and fresh grass. Around are the murmuring trees and fragrant flowers. And in the center is self-indulgent *me*, dreaming of the past or dreaming of the future, or just nuzzling my true love in my arms. This scenic effect is the key to everything. It places the situation afar off, so that we must visualize it as if through a frame and glass. Across that hazy distance the situation stands securely contained within itself, and we, in projecting ourselves into it, are safely protected from the real world.

How is it possible for people to enjoy this scenic version of nature, when at the top of their minds they also think of nature as a mechanical realm of blank matter? How can they follow both the dreaming poet and the hard-headed scientist at one and the same time? The reason is that in essence both viewpoints are identical. They both see nature as a realm with no dynamic reality of its own, with no value in terms of the experiences it imposes on men. It has value only for what human subjectivity can do to it, in the one case by the poetic exercise of wishful dreaming, in the other by the scientific exercise of technical reason. Indeed, it may be that the dreamer flourishes only through the authority of the scientist. Perhaps men feel free to abandon the reality principle in relation to nature only because the truth-seekers have assured them that nothing unexpected can happen there. Since that realm has no momentous possibilities of its own to threaten or exalt, let it be an unreal place of indolent bliss.

This conventional "enjoyment of nature,"—which is really

not at all an enjoyment of nature itself, but an evacuation of nature in a splurge of wish-fulfillment—is what Wallace Stevens abominates. He knows its subtle attraction, the peace of beautiful vistas,

> The obscure moon lighting an obscure world
> Of things that would never be quite expressed,
> Where you yourself were never quite yourself
> And did not want or have to be.

Yet he turns emphatically against this. What he finds in nature, and what he wants to open to his reader, is not a chiaroscuro world of half tones, quarter-things, and distant scenes, but

> The weight of primary noon,
> The A B C of being,
>
> The ruddy temper, the hammer
> Of red and blue, the hard sound—
> Steel against intimation—the sharp flash,
> The vital, arrogant, fatal, dominant X.[11]

Stevens, in other words, wants reality and not pleasure to be his controlling principle, and this leads him to his obscure style.

IV.

At one level, he completely discards the conventional techniques. He keeps as far away as possible from the dear old countryside. When trees or flowers or sky appear in his work, he takes great care to dissociate them from the atmosphere of the deep woods and blossoming sward. He gives them an appearance far different from the one they receive in the typical rural setting. His earliest work revels in the lush brillance of the Caribbean. Later he finds an even greater brilliance within the city. His bright blossoms are those of a bouquet that stands on

a living-room table.[12] His trees are the dogwoods along a subur-
ban street, where a woman is walking her pet dog.[13] His weather
is what he finds on the way to the bus,[14] or while driving at
night along the highway from Cornwall to Hartford,[15] or while
watching Negroes playing football in the park on a Sunday afternoon.[16]

Stevens' insistence on reality also means that he avoids the use
of distant scenes. He does not write to carry his readers to some
remote, self-contained haven of misty peace. He wants to make
them more aware of the concrete world that actually presses
upon their consciousness. He wants them to perceive that world
when it is too close and too enveloping to be looked at or talked
about according to some preset human scheme, whether scientific or artistic. That is why in each of his poems he goes out
of his way to disorganize his presentation of the place, and to
prevent his reader from imagining it as a scene. The "Late
Hymn from the Myrrh-Mountain" is typical. In rapid sequence
we are confronted with an unsnacked snood, stars over Neversink, a departed bird, a molten day, remembered constellations,
diamonds in the hair, and dry, brown grass. It is impossible to
fashion the conventional version of nature from this disorder.
Stevens has seen to it that the arranging mind cannot possibly
compose these ingredients into a far-off, restful scene.

To the extent that he moves at this first level and refuses to
follow the escapist conventions, Stevens will disturb many readers. How can one know how to react to a nature poem when it
does not offer the familiar comfort of rural vegetation? How can
one orient oneself to the subject of a poem, when no scene is
provided as a frame of reference and everything seems to hang
in a void?

Stevens, however, does not stop at this level of the problem.
Nature has not lost its dynamic presence simply because people
have objectified it as a scene. On the contrary, they have given
it this form because of their belief in static, three-dimensional
space. It has become a deeply engrained habit for men to take
what they receive by sensation, to recreate it imaginatively in
terms of solid objects that exist in an objective three-dimensional

world, and then to convince themselves that this objective realm is what they actually experience in the moment of sensation. Here, according to Stevens, is the root of the problem. As long as men do this, and insist that things are real only by existing away from them in external space, then the world will necessarily lose its dynamic immediacy.

In Stevens' style, the effort to keep things from falling into *any kind* of an external situation is more fundamental than his avoidance of rural places and scenic arrangements. If a tree or bird appears in his verse, it does so in the mode of immediacy, as a blurred "presence" rather than a clear-cut identifiable "object." He makes it surge into the reader's awareness with its own unmanageable dynamism, as something vital, arrogant, and flashing. Not objects in space, but objects at the moment of impact; not an external world to be looked at across a distance, but an enveloping world that engulfs a man's senses—these might be taken as the fundamental principles of his style. The reader's spatial imagination is deliberately and ruthlessly frustrated. Here nothing is identified as the familiar kind of object that men distill in their imaginations from a variety of experiences and that they find recorded in photographs. Here

> the used-to earth and sky, and the tree
> And cloud, the used-to tree and used-to cloud,
> Lose the old uses that they made of them,
> And they: these men, and earth and sky, inform
> Each other by sharp informations, sharp. . . .[17]

In the "Late Hymn from the Myrrh-Mountain" we can see how effectively Stevens is able to obstruct the spatial imagination and to prevent his reader from viewing anything at a distance. We should note that the words of the poem do not cause any difficulty. It uses an ordinary vocabulary and a simple, straightforward syntax. The difficulty is experienced wholly by the habit of trying to visualize how the objects presented might look if they stood out there in some particular space.

In the opening lines, for instance, nothing is described in such a way that we can form a picture of it. The stars do not shine on some recognizable vista, but on "all the brows of Neversink," whatever they are. The fireflies do not glow or flicker; they "acknowledge" the planets. The planets do not shine or wheel, but are simply "predestined to this night, this noise." Nothing is being visualized for us. The same thing is true of the next part of the poem. A day is described when summer begins to wane and to lose the full radiance that made it beautiful. The natural world at that moment is compared to a bird which still possesses vivid color and still has its wings spread out, but which is no longer in flight.

> Tomorrow will look like today,
>
> Will appear like it. But it will be an appearance,
> A shape left behind, with like wings spreading out,
>
> Brightly empowered with like colors, swarmingly,
> But not quite molten, not quite the fluid thing.

This analogy between day and bird is the heart of the poem, and yet note how it is presented. No effort is made to give a visual picture of summer beauty, with clouds and trees and flowers. Moreover, in the image, the bird as such is not presented to us and never named. We are given only an expansive evocation of swarming colors and outspread wings.

The reason for this is clear. The poem focuses our attention upon this summer night, not as a scene in space, but as an immediate presence. Stevens wants us to remember how waning summer meets us with its own urgent immediacy. He does not want us to absorb this image by trying to form in our minds a *picture* of a summer day, then trying to imagine the *picture* of some bird, and finally trying to make a comparison between them. This is not the *region of awareness* in which the poem moves. The image functions to set the summer days before us in the mode of immediate impact. In that moment we do not see flowers as such or trees as such, but only moving blotches of bright colors soaring into the sky. Yet this, as the image indicates, is exactly the appearance of a flying bird at the instant when it first breaks upon our awareness. We do not then see an external, clearly identifiable thing called "bird," which we have often met before, but simply a blur of winged color. Stevens designs his image to arouse in us a sense of summer in its dazzling immediacy, when under the pressure of light and color we are unable to externalize and picture the objects around us. If we do not let the image work in this domain, if we insist on trying to visualize an external world of definite items, where only days have seasons and only birds have wings, and where there can be no more than comparative similarities between them, then the image will only frustrate us.

Once the image has made its impact, we can understand how the poem is arranged stylistically. First comes the night, when there is neither sensory impact nor external world, but only the necessitated pinpoints of light that belong to stars and fireflies. Then, through the central image, we look back upon the season of full summer that is now passing, the season when all ordinary objects were dissolved in a kind of radiance. In the final lines, the character of the coming season is indicated. The world now ceases to besiege the mind with its swarming glow. Its life dries up. It loses its immense reality. It withdraws into the unreality of manageable distance. At last the mind can visualize it in objective space. At last the poet can portray it in the language of external description.

> The deer-grass is thin. The timothy is brown.
> The shadow of an external world comes near.

The point of the poem, then, cannot be found in anything that it tells us about the objective world. Its point lies wholly in its difficult *style*, in the very thing that most readers find troublesome. By means of this style the poem introduces us to three different relations between the mind and the surrounding world— an intellectual relation of abstractness (the present dark night), an ecstatic relation of immediacy (the passing dazzle of summer), and a prosaic relation of externality (the coming drab autumn). And in the course of this journey, it conveys a sense of how much of reality has disappeared in the final stage.

If we realize how completely the ordinary person relies on his spatial imagination to organize what he reads, we can appreciate why he finds Stevens' style so difficult and exasperating. It lacks the kind of order he knows, and therefore seems like a chaos. It deliberately gives him no external vantage point from which to organize things, not even a satisfactory title. To submit to its spell is like

> passing a boundary, floating without a head
> And naked, or almost so, into the grotesque
> Of being naked, or almost so, in a world

Of nakedness, in the company of the sun.[18]

In reading Stevens, it is useful to remember that he was not the first to frustrate the spatial imagination. In this he is consciously following the path already laid out by modern painting. Ever since the French impressionists exposed the artificiality of the world of external space and began to paint things, not as generalized objects, but exactly as they appeared to the eye in a single instant, painters have discarded the laws of perspective and the fixed framework of space. Some explored the dimension of color in experience, and discovered that individual colors as such, without reference to any particular external objects, make a definite kind of impact upon the consciousness. They can provoke resonances in the mind that go far deeper than anything it receives while visualizing three-dimensional things. Other painters probed the impact of pure forms, recognizing that in the experience of any object the eye grasps and the mind reacts to its general form long before its specific details are sorted out.

In any case, whatever their particular focus, all the modern artists have been opposed to the illusion of a self-contained space, not because they wanted to express their private emotions or to indulge in their fancies or to distort reality, but because they wanted to recover reality, "to render the image of what we see, even if it means forgetting everything that existed before us" (Cézanne). They were ruthlessly attacked. People could not understand why they did not paint things the way they "actually looked," that is, the way they looked in external space. "Try to make Pissarro understand," one French critic cried out in exasperation, "that trees are not violet, that the sky is not the color of fresh butter, that in no country do we see the things he paints, and that no intelligence can accept such aberrations!" The painters, however, knew better. They knew that this is exactly how things appear at a specific moment, before the intelligence has a chance to identify them and reduce them to their objective ordinariness. They knew that stereoscopic realism, by wrapping things up in a static, external space, not only falsifies experience, but has the fatal consequence of robbing the world of all its dynamic immediacy.

Tell Seurat [Van Gogh once wrote to his brother, Letter #418] that I should despair if my figures were correct, that I do not *want* them to be academically correct. Tell him that in my view, if you photograph a digger, he is sure to look as if he were not digging. Tell him that I adore Michelangelo's figures, even though the legs are certainly too long, the hips and the pelvic bones too large. Tell him that for me Millet and Lhermitte are the real artists, because they do not paint things as they are, traced in a dry, analytical way, but as they sense them. Tell him that my great longing is to learn to achieve those very inaccuracies, those deviations, remodelings and changes in reality, so that my works may be, yes, lies if you like—but truer than the literal truth.

Within the realm of painting this movement has succeeded. The old spatial "realism" has lots its grip, and many people have discovered a new kind of pictorial experience. But this has not yet occurred within their enjoyment of the written word. Insofar as their reading habits are concerned, they still expect every work to orient itself within some spatial framework. Stevens is the first to extend the painters' revolution to American poetry, and modern painting provides an excellent introduction to his work. As he himself wrote, "to a large extent, the problems of poets are the problems of painters, and poets must often turn to the literature of painting for a discussion of their own problems." [19]

We can guess what happens when the conventional, visualizing attitude tries to read Stevens. Marguerite Wilkinson will serve as an example. In her *New Voices: An Introduction to Contemporary Poetry*, she examines one of Stevens' early works, called "Tattoo." [20]

> The light is like a spider.
> It crawls over the water.
> It crawls over the edges of the snow.
> It crawls under your eyelids
> And spreads its webs there—
> Its two webs.
>
> The webs of your eyes
> Are fastened
> To the flesh and bones of you
> As to rafters or grass.
>
> There are filaments of your eyes
> On the surface of the water
> And in the edges of the snow.

The poem calls attention to the fact that in every act of seeing there is not only a visual experience of distant objects, but also a tactile experience of the light itself. Indeed, as we recognize whenever we come out of the dark, this tactile experience comes first. We feel the impact of the light before we see things in the light. The poem focuses on this tactile element, and explores it by means of three images. It speaks first of the shimmering, spidery effect of light on water or snow. It indicates that when this piercing light strikes the eye, it feels as if it were etching its way over the whole eyeball, and by its brightness were walling sight off from any contact with the familiar world. Then, under the image of two webs, the clinging, enveloping fingers of light are compared to the tissues that bind the eyeball to the eye socket and that are diagramed so vividly in biology textbooks. Finally, a third and quite different tactile analogy is provided by the title. The visual experience is like a tattoo, and the probing fingers of light that strike the eye are compared to the tattoo needle, which produces an image by repeatedly puncturing the skin.

In their total effect, these three images reinforce each other. They suggest that vision may not be just an automatic and secure contemplation of objects at a distance, an act in which the sovereign ego sets itself apart from the surrounding world and gazes where it will. Vision may involve a deep disquietude, an uneasy feeling that we are helplessly engrafted by light into the physical mesh of things, as a spider engulfs a fly. To be awakened and alerted by the poem, however, the reader must be willing to have his attention turned completely away from the second and obvious moment of sight, when the consciousness is absorbed in the world of objects. He must let the poem help him focus upon the first, infinitesimal moment, when light makes its tactile impact.

Miss Wilkinson, however, approaches the poem in the strictly conventional terms. Ignoring the title as of no help at all, she considers light and spiders as they appear at a distance, and tries to discover some points of resemblance between them. As we might expect, she finds none, and has to conclude that the poem is nothing but a clever trick.

> A spider is a small dark, rayed object moving in darts and jerks. Is light a spider in form, color, texture, movement, power? Do spiders *crawl* over water, over the edges of snow, under our eyelids? It sounds improbable. To read these lines thoughtfully is to be convinced that light is not like a spider. It is difficult to conceive of any interpretation of the poem that would reveal truth in this symbol.

This is exactly the complaint that the French critic made against the painter Pissarro: "in no country do we see the things he paints."

Miss Wilkinson accuses Stevens of "aesthetic insincerity" and "artistic immorality," and sets him in contrast to the "honesty" that she finds in Carl Sandburg's "Fog."

> The fog comes
> on little cat feet.
>
> It sits looking
> over harbor and city
> on silent haunches
> and then moves on.

These lines call up the *picture* of a fog moving in upon a city; they look at the scene from across a distance. According to Miss Wilkinson, this represents honest poetry. "The symbolism is daring, but it is quite true and has been truthfully felt."

In the same spirit, she also recommends the poem "Silver" by Walter de la Mare, which describes a moonlight scene.

> It is a color study [she explains], delighting us as a fine painting would. . . . Few poems of our day have so great a beauty of imagery. For every image is true. Anyone can see the same thing at the right place and time.

> Couched in his kennel, like a log,
> With paws of silver sleeps the dog;
> From their shadowy cote the white breasts peep
> Of doves in a silver-feathered sleep.

> This is all said in magical words. Millions of men and women and children have seen this silver symphony on moonlight nights. Now it is poetry.

Stevens' work is based on the premise that the lines by De la Mare are *not* poetry at all. It would be difficult to find verse which so perfectly illustrates the dishonesty and unreality that Stevens opposes. In the first place, contrary to Miss Wilkinson's last contention, very few people have ever seen such a scene as this. The co-presence of dogs and doves is not only an impossibility in the cities and suburb, but would be an oddity even in the country. In the second place, the actual experience of seeing things in moonlight does not at all happen as the poem claims. De la Mare assumes that if we were standing in the place described, each object would clearly show its identity, so that there would be no hesitation in naming this thing a dog and that a dove—each would simply be colored with prettifying light. In fact, a new light makes a new object to the senses, and anyone standing in this scene might have great difficulty in determining whether that silver shape was a dog or a bear, and whether those silver blobs were doves or blossoms. Far from being "true" to sensory experience, then, De la Mare has simply combined a set of trite rural objects, and doused them in unreal moonlight. The only place where these objects could appear as they do in this poem is not in the real moonlight, but in some calendar picture or Christmas card. In the third place, if Miss Wilkinson is correct, and millions of people are already habituated to thinking of moonlight scenes in this way, then why bother doing it in poetry? Poetry can open up new perceptions and explore the real world in its unfamiliar aspects. It need hardly justify itself by clinging to stale modes of experience, and presenting what "anyone" would see with no effort at the same time and place.

V.

Up to this point we have been considering the difficulties in Stevens' style, especially as they arise from his refusal to locate his subjects in external space. Stevens, of course, is not original in protesting against objectivized nature. Not only have there been such philosophers as Kant, Hegel, Bergson, and Whitehead, and the many movements in modern painting. Within poetry itself Stevens may be seen as carrying on the tradition of the English and American romantics. These men repudiated the scientific view that nature is an external realm from which the mind stands withdrawn and which it can only analyze and manipulate. They, too, wanted to celebrate the immediate impact of nature.

In Walt Whitman's words, they wanted above everything else to *vivify*, "to give ultimate vivification to facts, to science and to common lives, endowing them with the glows and glories and final illustriousness which belong to every real thing, and to real things only."

Within this romantic tradition, however, Stevens is a very distinctive figure, especially in terms of the "reality" that he finds touching men in nature. In order to examine this side of his work, we must no longer concern ourselves with the difficulties of his style, but inquire instead about what that style positively conveys.

It is important to recognize that Stevens' poetry deals almost exclusively with certain peculiar moments of experience. These are by no means exceptional moments; they happen to everyone and they happen often. The trouble is that most people take no notice of them. They are dismissed and forgotten as soon as they occur. Yet Stevens not only finds in them the subject for his poetry; he also believes that they are a genuine revelation of reality and a complete fulfillment of human life. To get some understanding of these moments, let us compare one of his earlier poems with one of his last.

In 1923, at the age of forty-four, he published his first book, with the title *Harmonium*. "The Curtains in the House of the Metaphysician" was one of the poems here.

> It comes about that the drifting of these curtains
> Is full of long motions; as the ponderous
> Deflations of distance; or as clouds
> Inseparable from their afternoons;
> Or the changing of light, the dropping
> Of the silence, wide sleep and solitude
> Of night, in which all motion
> Is beyond us, as the firmament,
> Up-rising and down-falling, bares
> The last largeness, bold to see.

If we judge by the opening lines, this seems to be a poem about drifting curtains and about the odd fancies that they might arouse. As it develops, however, it effects some radical changes.

In rapid sequence, we are shown other instances of the same long, drifting motion—the sweep of a rolling landscape, the slow progression of afternoon clouds, the shifting tones of sunlight during the day, and the gradual descent of darkness at night. This series of resemblances, it should be noted, does not serve to make the initial experience of house curtains more intense. On the contrary, it produces a genuine metamorphosis, leading our minds away from the curtains completely. What is kept vividly before us is the slow, drifting motion itself, as it is encountered in vistas, in clouds, in sunlight, and in night. Finally, at the end, this motion embraces the whole cosmos. The descent of night has become something else, the slow movement of the firmament. Though ignored in astronomy books, this dome beyond the stars dominates a person's concrete experience of dusk. At first, as the sun begins to set, this black dome seems to rise from the horizon and gather overhead. Then, when the last trace of sunlight disappears, it falls upon us, like an ultimate reality. Through the movement of the poem, the drifting curtains are turned into this up-rising and down-falling firmament. The ordinary house has become the enveloping cosmos, or, as the title playfully says, "the House of the Metaphysician."

This change in the scope of attention is accompanied by a change in the mode of consciousness. The style gradually loses its descriptive quality and becomes imagistic. Our attention is drawn away from the external world of clear-cut objects that stand over against us—curtains, vistas, clouds, etc. By the time we read of the night, we are made to think of how its darkness strikes us upon immediate impact, of how we sense its enveloping presence out of the corner of our eye, even while at the top of our minds we may still be examining its details and trying to locate it objectively under familiar labels. We are reminded of the instant when the night engulfs us like a total world. This is the same thing that happens in the "Late Hymn from the Myrrh-Mountain," where the object-less rhetoric of outspread wings and swarming colors dissolves all externality.

Finally, these shifts in the scope and region of awareness bring about a change in the quality of the emotions involved. What began as a minor and very specific feeling about drifting curtains has become nothing minor at all, but a momentary experience of the enveloping universe, a kind of total mood over the way in which the last horizons of reality are related to the self. As the imagination is led from the curtained room with its heavy ponderousness, into the open spaces of earth and sky, and finally to a point where "all motion is beyond us" and we stand in the presence of an ultimate immensity, there develops a growing sense of release and exultant invigoration. This is generated primarily in the changing rhythm of the sentence, but it comes into final focus in the last phrase, "bold to see."

These three changes—in scope of attention, mode of experience, and emotional quality—are produced quickly. This speed is actually the most important feature of the poem. Because each line moves rapidly into the next, and because the syntax puts everything within a single sentence and therefore within the sweep of a single thought, there is no sharp break between the initial response to the curtains and the final experience of the firmament. In fact, the poem gives the impression that the total awareness at the end was already dumbly present at the beginning, and only needed a little time to come to full consciousness. In other words, the poem does not portray the mind moving itself from one thing to another by its own inventiveness, but shows the mind being moved and being taken possession of by a strange awareness. In this sense, the poem gives the impression of responding to disclosures from reality, and not just of expressing the poet's own fancies.

If we turn now from the beginning to the end of Stevens' life, we come to his last group of poems, entitled *The Rock*, which he published in 1954 at the age of seventy-five. One of these is "Vacancy in the Park."

> March . . . Someone has walked across the snow,
> Someone looking for he knows not what.
>
> It is like a boat that has pulled away
> From a shore at night and disappeared.

It is like a guitar left on a table
By a woman, who has forgotten it.

It is like the feeling of a man
Come back to see a certain house.

The four winds blow through the rustic arbor,
Under its mattresses of vines.

There are obvious differences between this and the preceding poem. The pace here is slower and more deliberate. The instances of vacancy do not flow swiftly upon each other, but each occupies its own stanza, completes itself within its own sentence, and has its own weight. There is also a different progression of instances, not outward from a bit of household furnishing to the dome of the universe, but self-ward. The reader is shown a series of places from which *other* people have departed. Then suddenly the whole perspective is changed, and he is confronted with an experience of *his own* total absence, like a man looking at the house where he once lived but from which every trace of his own life has now been obliterated. This shift of perspective to oneself is what produces the effect of enveloping immediacy in the poem.

What is significant about the two poems, however, is their fundamental similarity, in spite of the interval of thirty-one years that separates them. A quality seen in some object presses upon the imagination and becomes immediately felt—a slow, drifting motion in the one case, and a sense that some person has departed in the other. Then, by means of a series of resemblances, this quality becomes a characteristic of the whole world, which presses upon the consciousness like an enveloping atmosphere.

A great number of Stevens' poems are built around this same pattern. The reader is carried from some quiet detail in the scene out there to an intense experience of the surrounding world. This movement constitutes the element of surprise, the atmosphere of dynamic change on which Stevens depends. Of course, he does not often achieve this movement by using a simple sequence of resemblances (as . . . as . . . as . . .). He has no standard technique that he automatically turns on whenever he wants to produce a poem. "All poetry," he says, "is experimental," [21] and every poem, a new experiment. Yet all his variety serves the same end, to elaborate this sort of momentary experience, when the whole world suddenly engulfs the consciousness.

Three examples will indicate the variety in Stevens' portrayal of these moments.

1. In "No Possum, No Sop, No Taters" he begins with a scene. He builds up the picture of a winter world where blank cold has stunted and strangled every trace of life.

> He is not here, the old sun,
> As absent as if we were asleep.
>
> The field is frozen. The leaves are dry.
> Bad is final in this light.
>
> In this bleak air the broken stalks
> Have arms without hands. They have trunks
>
> Without legs or, for that, without heads.
> They have heads in which a captive cry
>
> Is merely the moving of a tongue.
> Snow sparkles like eyesight falling to earth,
>
> Like seeing fallen brightly away.
> The leaves hop, scraping on the ground.
>
> It is deep January. The sky is hard.
> The stalks are firmly rooted in ice.

Yet just then, as these accumulated details envelop the mind with a sense of the killing cold and as this quality is crystallized in the final image of ice encasing the broken stalks, the unexpected happens. The descriptive scene dissolves, and in its place we encounter in quick succession references to an act of speech, to an ultimate knowledge of the good, and to the loss of solitude.

> It is deep January. The sky is hard.
> The stalks are firmly rooted in ice.

It is in this solitude, a syllable,
Out of these gawky flitterings,

Intones its single emptiness,
The savagest hollow of winter-sound.

It is here, in this bad, that we reach
The last purity of the knowledge of good.

The crow looks rusty as he rises up.
Bright is the malice in his eye . . .

One joins him there for company,
But at a distance, in another tree.

It is as if, through all the scenic details accumulated in the first part of the poem, the engulfing whole suddenly steps forth and touches the self. The self knows the presence of some kind of fullness, of a higher order of reality. The cold, instead of being an agent of death, has become a precious vehicle for communication and contact. The self here has touched more than a cold world. The spectacle of bad things out there dissolves for an instant into a single, all-embracing syllable, which does not crush the self, as might be expected, but fills it with a strange purity of knowledge. This peculiar contact and knowledge are what bring relief from the oppressive solitude. As one who hears the speech of the enveloping whole and becomes absorbed by it, the human self feels a kinship with the other creatures submerged in ice, and sees even the malicious crow in a new way.

2. In contrast to this first poem, "Girl in a Nightgown" concentrates, not upon a scene, but upon a single detail, and issues in a vision of upheaval rather than of frozen barrenness. A girl ready for bed stands at the window. At first, in her childlike way, she enjoys the protective silence and immensity of the darkness, and hears the thunder only as an item in the background. But the distant booming begins to grip her attention, and suddenly she feels that this violence is actually the fundamental reality behind all things. The unshakable and protective night has been shattered. The possibility of peaceful sleep has disappeared. She begins to bear the burden of adult imagination.

Lights out. Shades up.
A look at the weather.
There has been a booming all the spring,
A refrain from the end of the boulevards.

This is the silence of night,
This is what could not be shaken,
Full of stars and the images of stars—
And that booming wintry and dull,

Like a tottering, a falling and an end,
Again and again, always there,
Massive drums and leaden trumpets,
Perceived by feeling instead of sense,

A revolution of things colliding.
Phrases! But of fear and of fate.
The night should be warm and fluters' fortune
Should play in the trees when morning comes.

Once it was, the repose of night,
Was a place, strong place, in which to sleep.
It is shaken now. It will burst into flames,
Either now or tomorrow or the day after that.

3. Quite a different experiment is pursued in "The House
Was Quiet and the World Was Calm."

The house was quiet and the world was calm.
The reader became the book; and summer night

Was like the conscious being of the book.
The house was quiet and the world was calm.

The words were spoken as if there was no book,
Except that the reader leaned above the page,

Wanted to lean, wanted much most to be
The scholar to whom his book is true, to whom

The summer night is like a perfection of thought.
The house was quiet because it had to be.

The quiet was part of the meaning, part of the mind:
The access of perfection to the page.

And the world was calm. The truth in a calm world,
In which there is no other meaning, itself

Is calm, itself is summer and night, itself
Is the reader leaning late and reading there.

Here the quality immediately felt is not bitter coldness or violence, but the almost palpable quietness felt late at night, after
all the noises outside have died away and everyone else in the
house has gone to bed. The initial detail is the act of reading a
book, itself an act of interior quietness. The poem seeks to show
that the reader's leaning effort to live outside himself and in the
book is actually an effort to reach a calm world, a world of enveloping calmness in which there is no other meaning but the
calmness itself. This transformation is achieved primarily by
means of cadenced repetition. The two phrases "the house was
quiet," "the world was calm" keep recurring like an ever present
security. At first they simply sketch out the background atmosphere—the scene—in which the reading occurs. As they are repeated, however, they become central, until at the end they dominate everything, even references to the reader and his book.
Calmness has become the reality of the whole cosmos, and all
detailed objects are simply vessels of its presence.

These three poems all involve different devices and all make
heavy demands upon the reader's imagination. Yet the experiences that control them—what Stevens calls "the moments of
enlargement"—are known to everyone. One walks down a familiar street to the office for a business appointment. Suddenly,
the sunlight takes on a peculiar richness, covering the pavement
and cars and buildings with a blanket of gold. For an instant
the familiar scene has dissolved into something new and strange.
The workaday job and the waiting appointment are forgotten.
The consciousness is completely absorbed in wonder. Then, just
as suddenly, the sunlight regains its ordinary tones. The gold
world vanishes without a trace, leaving the familiar street and

the job obligations. One shrugs one's shoulders and hurries on. It must have been a trick of the mind.

Or again, on a hot summer night, the light breeze that has been blowing since dusk dies away. In the ensuing stillness, the heat seems to move in with crushing force. The place and the time in their familiar orientation are blotted out. They have been completely filled with the heavy heat, so that momentarily they seem to have lost all their own reality. It does not last, of course. A car drives by or a voice calls from the house, and we are brought back to normal.

Or again, one strolls through the public garden on a fine day in May, feeling the burst of life in everything. Ahead down the walk, a girl laughs and spins lightly around, so that her bell skirt fills and rises, and its large black and white squares flash in the sunlight. Then it is gone. One realizes with some irritation that a baby is screeching on the grass, that the cigarette is smoked through, that the girl is really a thin, forlorn creature. But for an instant the world in all its zing was completely present. That gay laugh and that bright swirling skirt completed the moment, and brought into full focus the exhilaration of life and color that had been hanging in the air all morning.

In these moments the world steps forth from behind its externality. It takes on a strange intensity, alive with unexpected magnitudes. It envelops the self, so that a man forgets that he exists inside his skin and that the world is an external realm out there, which he must look at across a distance. For an instant his consciousness blends with his surroundings. He has become one with the glory that rolls around him, with the whole transfigured world that gathers him into itself. He experiences a moment of ecstasy.

These experiences are known to everyone. The trouble is that they are too fleeting. They cannot be caught by ordinary thought or expressed by ordinary speech. Therefore no one takes them seriously. To people caught up in obligations and appointments, they are not worth noticing.

For Stevens, however, these experiences are not at all unimportant. They represent a peculiar encounter between man and the world, a life-giving instant of reconciliation and openness. The world steps forward with a radiance that it never has when it lies before us as an objective realm. An analogy may help us to see this aspect of these moments. Imagine a person who has lived his whole life in a completely enclosed room, surrounded by four unbroken walls and given illumination only by an artificial light. Now suppose that the walls and ceiling and floor of that enclosed room suddenly become transparent. Without warning the person inside is confronted by the huge expanses of earth and sky, and by the dazzling brilliance of sunlight. For the first time he sees fields and hills stretching to the horizon. He gazes at towering clouds and endless blue. He watches the ever changing panorama of color and shade. He is swallowed up in a new and unbelievable immensity. His room—that box of space enclosed by six flat surfaces—no longer exists as his frame of reference. Though he is still in the room, now the vast outdoors has become his real world. His feelings and his thoughts are wrenched out of their old narrow confines. His mind now flows outward through this vastness, and experiences the strange freedom of being able to stretch itself unimpeded. The room is simply the transparent place where the immensity of space envelops him.

For Stevens, this is precisely the sort of thing that happens in the moments which he portrays in his poems, in what I shall call the "engulfing moments." It is not space that men meet here, but a magnificence, a dazzle, a peculiar intensification in the reality of things. The whole world is momentarily transfigured. In the blaze of summer, a man turned his head to see a single spruce tree, and

> suddenly,
> The tree stood dazzling in the air
>
> And blue broke on him from the sun,
> A bullioned blue, a blue abulge,
>
> Like daylight, with time's bellishings,
> And sensuous summer stood full-height.[22]

This is the fullness discovered in the engulfing moments. Insofar as people see their relationship to the world in terms of space, insofar as they exist only as solid objects groping for contact with other solid objects, reality is dull routine. Their experience reaches no further than to objective surfaces, and is as limited as that of the man in the enclosed room. In the fleeting moments that Stevens explores, however, the remote external world suddenly becomes immediately present. The hard surface of things drops away. A person no longer exists in three-dimensional space. Through the winter cold, or the booming thunder, or the quietness of night, an enveloping enormity steps forth, pervading the whole world. For an instant he forgets the projects with which he tries to handle his environment. He ceases looking at the world. He seems to be flowing through it, touching all its edges at once. There are no adequate words for the glory that momentarily engulfs him. He is caught up in a dazzle "Of Bright & Blue Birds & the Gala Sun."

> Some things, niño, some things are like this,
> That instantly and in themselves they are gay
> And you and I are such things, O most miserable . . .
>
> For a moment they are gay and are a part
> Of an element, the exactest element for us,
> In which we pronounce joy like a word of our own.

The 378 poems we have from Stevens might almost be read as accounts of 378 fleeting experiences of this kind. They happen in every conceivable situation, and from the most unlikely sources. They may be occasioned by a bouquet of roses or an empty jar, by a ruined church or a deserted farm, by swans flying or eagles diving or polo ponies practicing or children picnicking. They may occur at the moment of dreaming or at the moment of waking; in the depths of love, in the midst of war, or in the shadow of death; while hearing an oboe, or walking by a river, or swimming in a stream, or just eating peaches— touching them, smelling them, tasting them "with my whole body," absorbing them "as the Angevine/Absorbs Anjou." [23] In

Stevens' work they often come in connection with the extremes of climate. Any number of his poems are devoted to the dead of winter or the height of summer, and especially to the instant when this maximum intensity of weather begins to arrive or pass away.

Above all, there is the magic of sunlight—at dawn, at noon, in the late afternoon, and at dusk, in summer dazzle and winter dullness, filling a garden or covering a nation or shimmering on an ocean or touching a glass of water. It showers the earth with an ever changing sheen of color and brightness.

> The sun is half the world, half everything,
> The bodiless half. There is always this bodiless half,
> This illumination, this elevation.[24]

Normally we think of sunlight as the basis for our objective experience. It illuminates the external world and enables us to see objects as distant, self-contained entities occupying humdrum space. However, the sunlight that does this is not the sunlight that Stevens describes, not the sunlight of immediate experience. It is an objective medium that we try to ignore in order to see the objects lying "out there." In the sunlight of immediate experience, however, there are no clearly identified objects, no "external" universe of static solidity. The first instants of vision offer us a perpetually strange world of dynamic shapes and flowing surfaces. Although the human mind usually trains itself not to notice this first instant, Stevens finds it an inexhaustible source for the fleeting experiences that concern him.

VI.

How is it possible for a poet like Stevens to notice these moments in so many places? It is a matter of breaking free from certain habits with which our culture trains the mind to deal with its experience. In other words, it is a matter of discipline—not a discipline of the body or of the will or of the reflective reason, but a discipline of the mind's first act of attention, training it to become aware of a level or kind of experience that it usually ignores. In order to produce his poetry, Stevens had to free himself from the habit of looking at the world only as a realm of external objects, and of immediately converting every experience into a withdrawn consideration of three-dimensional space. He had to learn how to hold his attention upon an earlier stage of awareness, before the mind had begun its process of objectivizing and classifying, when it was still only aware of its situation as an enveloping presence. This discipline is what Stevens himself calls breaking free from "the tyranny of the eye," since the eye is the organ through which the mind establishes an objective distance between itself and the world.

Stevens tells us that it was from the painters that he learned this discipline. A painter's task is not simply to notice the external world with photographic precision, but to learn how to see things in terms of "composition." Leo Stein gives a striking account of this process.

I put on the table a plate of the kind common in Italy, an earthenware plate with a simple pattern in color, and this I looked at every day for minutes or for hours. I had in mind to see it as a picture, and waited for it to become one. In time it did. The change came suddenly when the plate as an inventorial object, one made up of parts that could be separately listed, a certain shape, certain colors applied to it, and so on, went over into a composition to which all these elements were merely contributory. The painted composition on the plate ceased to be *on* it but became part of a larger composition which was the plate as a whole. I had made a beginning at seeing pictorially.

What had been begun was carried out in all directions. I wanted to be able to see anything *as* a composition and found that it was possible to do this. I tried it on everything from a scrap of paper torn from the corner of a sheet to a line of trees extending half a mile into the distance; and I found that with practice seeing pictures was possible everywhere.[25]

In Stein's usage here, "composition" does not mean the way in which a painter can manipulate lines and colors within a frame, so as to produce a pleasing picture for a museum. It is the way in which *something arranges itself* in the painter's experience, when it ceases to be an "inventorial object" and becomes a vital presence, when the jumble of accidental qualities that mark it are no longer accidental but belong to a pervasive whole.

"Composition" in this sense is exactly the habit that Stevens has perfected. In his poems the individual items do not exist with their own separate reality and meaning. In "The Curtains in the House of the Metaphysician," the curtains, the clouds, and the falling darkness have become ingredients of an enveloping totality, parts of a composition. The same with the footprints, forgotten guitar, and deserted house in "Vacancy." The individual things actualize the enveloping atmosphere of some moment as it grips the mind. In terms of the technique Stein describes, we might say that in these poems Stevens focused his attention upon the drifting curtain and the retreating footprints until he was able to see them "pictorially," until they lost their own reality and became contributory parts of a pervasive whole.

Every item in Stevens' poems functions in this non-objective, compositional way. What is important is not its normal function or traditional associations, but its place in one of these fleeting moments when the world suddenly envelops a man and the man finds himself flowing out into a radiant world. Then it does not exist in its own right but as the vessel of an enveloping presence, as part of a larger whole.

The other habit of mind which has no place in Stevens' verse and from which he learned to break free concerns the element of change. Usually when someone speaks of having an "experience," we take this to mean that his consciousness gained some kind of stable contact with a fragment of reality. To be sure, he had this experience directly only for a moment perhaps. But its genuineness lies in the fact that it gave his mind a secure and recoverable hold on some object. He no longer has to depend on direct experience. Having isolated and named this bit of the world, and having stored it in his memory, he is now able to recall it at will. He can hold it steadily before his mind whenever he wishes.

The engulfing moments that absorb Stevens are not "experiences" in this ordinary sense. They are too elusive, too sudden. They are gone even before the mind has a chance to realize their presence. And what they may present leaves no reassuring trace afterward in the objective world. Properly speaking, then, the content of these engulfing moments never stands before the mind for a long enough instant to be given static consideration. It is known and remembered only in terms of its approach and departure. It is a fleeting experience by its very essence.

In this connection, Stevens had to discipline his mind to rest in the fluidity of this experience, and not to strain after some content that he could fix before his gaze. And he had to carry this same discipline into his style. He could not falsify the moment with his words. He could not abstract it from the swift flow of its approach and withdrawal, so as to let its content stand before his reader's imagination with static clarity. In his choice of words and sentence structure, he could never once disregard *how* this enveloping presence was encountered, always as an unmanageably fleeting impression.

That is why, in the different poems given above, we find it difficult to get our bearings. Stevens' primary concern is not to clarify the content of these engulfing moments, but to catch their speed, to portray them in flight. A poem, he says, should be a meteor, or a pheasant disappearing into the bush.[26] This accounts for many of the peculiar features in his style—the general blurriness, the lack of any clear context, the swift movement of association and imagery, the unpausing syntax. He is not interested in the content, but only in the change which the engulfing moments bring. It is only "the instant of change," he writes, that is the poem.[27]

However, while this loyalty to change may cause him to fashion a "difficult" style, it also gives his verse a refreshing authenticity. I am thinking especially of those hymns to the glory of nature written during the last two centuries. At one extreme we have the complex suggestiveness of Shelley's "Mt. Blanc"

(1816), which contrasts the soaring stillness of the mountain with the savage scenery of the surrounding glaciers.

> Far, far above, piercing the infinite sky,
> Mont Blanc appears,—still, snowy, and serene—
> Its subject mountains their unearthly forms
> Pile around it, ice and rock; broad vales between
> Of frozen floods, unfathomable deeps,
> Blue as the overhanging heaven, that spread
> And wind among the accumulated steeps;
> A desert peopled by the storms alone,
> Save when the eagle brings some hunter's bone,
> And the wolf tracks her there—how hideously
> Its shapes are heaped around! rude, bare, and high,
> Ghastly, and scarred, and riven.

At the other extreme we have such folk verse as Robert Service's "The Spell of the Yukon" (1907).

> The winter! the brightness that blinds you,
>   The white land locked tight as a drum,
> The cold fear that follows and finds you,
>   The silence that bludgeons you dumb.
> The snows that are older than history,
>   The woods where the weird shadows slant;
> The stillness, the moonlight, the mystery,
>   I've bade 'em good-by—but I can't.

Both of these poems portray a richness and immensity in nature that might be compared to Stevens' engulfing moments. Yet both present that immensity as if it were the static property of some actual place in the external world. Both give the impression that we only have to travel the necessary miles and look at that real mountain or that real winter wasteland in order to recover this experience. In their language both poems *hold* a scene steadily before our minds, so that we can relish it. At this level, therefore, we find that they are easy to follow. Yet precisely for that reason, we also know that both are false. For such grandeur as they portray is never just part of the scenery. It depends on all kinds of accidental factors, such as the tone of the sunlight or the momentary shape of one's personal anxieties, and the experience of it is always momentary. If a person had a miserable cold in his head, he might look at Mt. Blanc for days and never be gripped by its vast and inaccessible tranquility. And should he attain this perception, it would be only for an instant. He would not thereafter always see Mt. Blanc in a heightened way. In fact his impression would have been so fleeting that he might soon begin to wonder whether he hadn't been imagining things, and he would have great difficulty finding words to convey what he had seen to another person.

In other words, there is a certain elusiveness in the experience, and because Stevens refuses to conceal this, because he never lets his words show the engulfing moment to be anything but a flash, something seen only for an instant out of the corner of the eye, his verse is authentic. The difficulties of his style re-actualize an invaluable aspect of immediate exprience itself. In his view, in fact, writers and readers who prefer a static vision of Mt. Blanc or the Yukon do not want poetry at all. They want prose. For prose is designed precisely to abstract the content of experience away from all flux and change. It functions to place every detail against a stationary background, or "context," and thus gives an aura of stability to everything that it presents. It proceeds slowly and methodically, enabling the reader to secure a more static gaze of the world.

This prose habit, then, is that from which Stevens freed his mind and his pen. By a long labor of trial and error, he found a way of avoiding the prose habits of speech, and of preventing stationary backgrounds and solid objects and magnificient scenes from creeping into his work. He learned not even to look *at* the engulfing moment itself, as if it were only a local phenomenon within a larger and essentially static universe. He let his verse be completely responsive to those moments, as they flash swiftly by the consciousness.

VII.

There is still one more aspect of these moments that Stevens' poetry calls to our attention. It is the quality of *intensity* with which they endow the whole world. Stevens recognizes that, contrary to the assumptions behind much scenic art, this intensity cannot be attributed to the spatial or physical qualities of a situation. It is as if some higher level of reality had momentarily filled the world. When golden sunlight suddenly converts the dirty city street into a strange wonderland of bright forms, and for an instant we are oblivious of time and place and duties, we do not seem to be taking in the objective properties of the scene around us. The automobiles and buildings have ceased to be there in their own right. They have lost their distinct, three-dimensional identities. They now seem to be nothing but vessels of some pervasive dazzle, as if a new presence filled them. They are still real, but in a wholly different way, alive with some surging glory rather than weighted by their own heaviness.

The effort to recognize and articulate this aspect of the moment has been the center of Stevens' attention since 1937, when "The Man in the Blue Guitar" appeared. It has figured in many of the poems given above. The drifting curtains in "the House of the Metaphysician" or the thunder at the end of the boulevards for the young girl not only cause the world to envelop the consciousness. They also appear charged by a power that surges from beyond the world of their normal, individual identities. In one of Stevens' favorite images, these poems make it seem that in the moment of immediacy "a shapeless giant" forces itself upward through the curtains or the thunder, and makes its presence felt.

Usually Stevens speaks of this transformation as a "metaphysical" event, in the technical sense of that word. A new and ultimate dimension of reality actually appears and fills everything with its own dazzling richness. The world of ordinary experience, of solid objects and ongoing routine, is revealed to be unreal. In many of his poems he calls this ultimate dimension "major reality," or "being itself." In this way he emphasizes how in the engulfing moment things not only have a different appearance, but seem to be real with a different kind of reality. For instance, they do not confront the mind as if they existed simply in terms of their occupation of space. They seem to belong to a more exalted order. They become nothing but vessels of radiance, magnified far beyond their ordinary status. The drifting curtains are media of some ultimate—"The last largeness, bold to see." For the girl the distant thunder becomes a metaphysical shaking. "Major reality" is Stevens' name for this transfiguring presence. When it shows itself in these momentary flashes, it empties things of their own separate, self-enclosed identity, not to make them vanish altogether, but to fill them with its own glory, with "The weight of primary noon."

> It was everything being more real, himself
> At the center of reality, seeing it.
> It was everything bulging and blazing and big in
>   itself,
> The blue of the rug, the portrait of Vidal,
> . . . the chairs.[28]

Stevens takes great pains in his poetry to make clear that this "major reality" is not some conceptual hypothesis that his rational mind has created to explain certain facts. He also emphasizes that it is not "reality" in the ordinary sense of the word, a self-contained being out there. It has no physical or visible dimensions of its own; it is simply the intensification of the physical world. It cannot be detected by any instrument that records physical lights and sounds. The girl in the nightgown may suddenly be engulfed by an ultimate shaking, but a microphone beside her would continue to hear only the thunder at the end of the boulevards. This does not mean that what the girl encounters here is unreal, but that it is too real, too immensely engulfing for any physical instrument. It is present only as that fleeting radiance which transfigures the world, but it then shows its incomparable power over all things. "There is," says Stevens, "a reality of or within or beneath the surface of reality," [29] and this is what comes forth in these special moments.

For Stevens, then, the engulfing moment is by no means simply an occasion when the usually distant and static world suddenly becomes immediate. In that state of immediacy, it is not the world itself at all, but *a reality of a higher order* that grips the mind. That is why, in trying to indicate the presence of this higher reality, he compares the moment to two other experiences: to the discovery that vast forces are surging under the surface of the world, and to the encounter with death.

In his poems Stevens makes use of almost every type of subsurface awareness that can be imagined. The moment, he says, is like hearing subterranean rumbles and quakings beneath the busy, active noise of individual things. Or it is like walking over ocean ice and feeling the tremendous tidal undulations underneath. Or it is like standing outdoors and encountering a giant in the fields and hills and sky, a "shapeless giant" without a body, writhing with a gigantic life of its own. Or it is like gazing at the surface of a flowing river. There we can see the images of buildings and trees. But we know that we are not looking at "real" objects in their solid externality. Because of the way they twist and ripple, we know that they are merely images, relatively unreal compared to the massive depth of water that is flowing underneath them. That is exactly how the engulfing moment imposes itself.[30] The world ceases to be a hard, impenetrable surface. Individual objects lose their static distance. They sway and ripple, and in that way they betray the presence of a vast metaphysical river that runs beneath their surface,

> The swarthy water
> That flows round the earth and through the skies,
> Twisting among the universal spaces.[31]

While these images portray the moment in terms of a reality beyond the surface of reality, they do not convey the radical otherness of what is involved. Stevens emphasizes this aspect when he identifies the moment with the immanence of death.

The prospect of death may be experienced as the approach of a great, invisible unknown, which will envelop us and shatter or transfigure the solid, three-dimensional world in which we have habitually lived. As such it becomes for Stevens an image of the engulfing moment.

In "Page from a Tale," for instance, a boy sits at night beside the frozen sea, huddled near his fire and listening to the wind. He thinks of the crippled ship that lies just out from shore, bound in the ice. He knows that it will soon be dawn, and that the people trapped on board will then begin their treacherous walk across the ice toward land. He imagines how the sun will appear to them then, the sun that can dissolve the one solid surface that holds them in this world. It will no longer be the ordinary sun, bringing back a familiar landscape. If it rises bright and clear, it will disclose within itself a new immensity, perhaps never before detected by these people, a power to choke the atmosphere, rend the ice, melt Arcturus, and annihilate the only world they have known. Yet this power is not physical but metaphysical, "beyond the habit of sense." Thus, in the immanence of death, major reality steps forth as something wholly other than the familiar world.

In another poem Stevens pictures Santayana in his old age, living as he did in a convent in Rome, cared for by nuns and awaiting death. Again the immanence of death is presented as an encounter with major reality, although here it brings exaltation rather than anguish.

> On the threshold of heaven, the figures in the street
> Become the figures of heaven, the majestic movement
> Of men growing small in the distances of space,
> Singing, with smaller and still smaller sound.
>
> .   .   .   .
>
> How easily the blown banners change to wings . . .
> Things dark on the horizons of perception,
> Become accompaniments of fortune, but
> Of the fortune of the spirit, beyond the eye,
> Not of its sphere, and yet not far beyond.

> . . . The newsboys' muttering
> Becomes another murmuring; the smell
> Of medicine, a fragrantness not to be spoiled . . .[32]

Over everything hangs the immanence of a new being, "a portent/On the chair, a moving transparence on the nuns," everything moving beyond itself, beyond its visible reality toward the invisible fullness that is approaching, beyond the eye but not too far beyond, everything reaching

> To join a hovering excellence, to escape
> From fire and to be part only of that of which
>
> Fire is a symbol: the celestial possible.

The spirit of the old man, too, is reaching,

> In the warmth of your bed, at the edge of your
>   chair, alive
> Yet living in two worlds, impenitent
> As to one, and, as to one, most penitent,
> Impatient for the grandeur that you need
>
> In so much misery.

These instances will give some indication of how Stevens reveals the transcendent quality in the engulfing moment. For him, it is not enough to break up the mental picture of an external, three-dimensional world and recover the flavor of immediate experience. Having recovered contact with immediacy, Stevens believes that the artist must then go on and articulate the shapeless giant, the metaphysical dithering, the more than visible blaze that discloses itself there. He must not be put off by current intellectual dogmas about what reality is or what sorts of experience are possible. In exploring immediate experience, he must be completely realistic, and insofar as he encounters "a reality of or within or beneath the surface of reality," he must celebrate its presence.

Let's see the very thing and nothing else.
Let's see it with the hottest fire of sight.
Burn everything not part of it to ash.

Trace the gold sun about the whitened sky
Without evasion by a single metaphor.
Look at it in its essential barrenness
And say this, this is the centre that I seek.[33]

The poet must not reproduce the pretty, sensible qualities of
the sun, when in it he is confronted by an intensity of a different order, by an "essential barrenness" that transcends all colors.
He must not arbitrarily limit himself to portraying just the physical weather in the impressionist fashion, but must sing of "the
giant of the weather," that is, of the invisible immensity which
is sensed to be surging through the weather. In the enormous
tumbling of clouds in the morning sky, it is his calling to declare
the more than visible which has become visible there. As Stevens
says in one striking expression, "the poet is the priest of the
invisible." [34] He celebrates those moments when the visible is
exalted by a peculiar intensity from beyond. He teaches men to
recognize the paradise that comes to them in the here and now.

VIII.

Because Stevens describes the engulfing moments as a new
kind of reality with words that come from the study of metaphysics, he is sometimes called a philosophic poet. This charac-
terization is bound to be misleading. Stevens has no interest
whatever in explaining things to the satisfaction of the rational
mind, or in developing a comprehensive account of experience.
He locates the poet within the realm of sense rather than of
abstract thought. "Poetry," he says, "has to be something more
than a conception of the mind. It has to be a revelation of
nature. Conceptions are artificial. Perceptions are essential." [35]

Stevens' real concern has an altogether different direction. He
explores the question of reality, not in the interests of reason,

but with respect to the tenor, or style, of life that different modes of reality draw forth from men. He is interested in what might be called *the feel of the world* upon the human consciousness, and in the fact that men have their whole behavior and personalities shaped by that feel. In particular, he wants to dispel "the cloak of heaviness" which lies over things in the external world, and which, he believes, oppresses the human spirit. By contrast everything in the engulfing moment has an airy and radiant lightness. If this latter represents the true and fundamental condition of reality, then men no longer need to feel that they are doomed to contend with a world of heavy, solid objects. In short, the engulfing moments have for Stevens a *redemptive* significance for human life, provided that they are seen in all their metaphysical importance.

Stevens points to many outer aspects of life to show what he means by this "cloak of heaviness." There is, for instance, the pressure of moral codes. These bind men to certain rigid patterns of attitude and behavior. They stifle all changeable spontaneity in the name of approved postures and irrevocable obligations. Their aim is to give a person "character," so that all his actions will be utterly reliable, utterly predictable. They exterminate his liveliness, in the interests of making him moral.

Again, there is the congestion of people in the modern city. There can be no such thing as privacy with the newspapers and telephones. At all times a man is open and defenseless against the intrusion of strangers. Everywhere they press against him with the weight of their voices and the urgency of their fears.

> If fifty private houses were built in New York this year, it would be a phenomenon. We no longer live in homes, but in housing projects, and that is so whether the project is literally a project or a club, a dormitory, a camp, or an apartment in River House. It is not only that there are more of us and that we are actually close together. We are closer together in every way. We lie in bed and listen to a broadcast from Cairo, and so on. There is no distance. We are intimate with people we have never seen and, unhappily, they are intimate with us.[86]

Still again, there is what Stevens calls the ceaseless concussion of daily events, "the pressure of the contemporaneous." [37] This, he feels, is a peculiarly modern torment, which he explains by contrast to the life he remembers from his youth. "In those days the seas were full of yachts and the yachts were full of millionaires. It was a time when only maniacs had disturbing things to say." There were Currier and Ives prints, and disasters seemed like purely local oddities. That world has now been taken down and tucked away like a stage setting. Today we look upon crisis as the normal condition. "We are preoccupied with events," he writes, "even when we do not observe them closely. We have a sense of upheaval. We feel threatened." It is not just that there are so many events happening so quickly that we cannot handle them, cannot tranquilize them in our minds. This is certainly true. In addition, however, events today seem to have a great violence that somehow touches us directly. We hear of a revolution in Syria or an air crash in Bolivia as if it happened in our very presence and were threatening something in our own lives. The pressure of the contemporaneous shakes us constantly, and tranquility has become an almost unknown state of mind.

These are some of the outer aspects of life that Stevens associates with weight and heaviness. Had he gone no further with the problem, he would probably have taken the obvious solution. Since the misery of life comes from the outer conditions of city life, let us remove these conditions. Let us go to the rural fields and sylvan glens. Stevens would probably have joined the general flight of poetry to the country. But he saw that the difficulty really lay, not in the circumstances men see around them, but in *their judgment about what makes these circumstances real,* in the kind of experiences in which they think reality is showing its essential character. For Stevens, then, people find the modern city oppressive, not because they live there, but because they equate reality with a static and highly rationalized level of their experience—with the world as an objectified realm of solid entities. They are convinced that something is real only to the extent that it belongs to this "objective" world, and possesses some heavy being of its own. They completely dismiss all fleeting experiences. If something does not stand steadily over against them, they assume that it is a mental fancy. They equate reality with that which endures, with that which does not keep dissolving into something else, with that which possesses a minimum of static, stonelike permanence.

Stevens observes how this judgment about reality operates in every corner of modern life. People want their world to be built out of indestructible particles. They want their knowledge to be grounded on solid facts. They want their security to be guaranteed by invincible weapons and impregnable defences. Above all, they imagine their gods in this same way. Since to be real means to be heavy and static, to be supremely real is to be supremely heavy and supremely static. And so men worship a God who has eternal, immovable, self-contained absoluteness. Their God not only does not change or move, but by His own inner nature He cannot change or move. Mercurial activity can have no place in His existence; His divinity lies in His unlimited heaviness. And alongside of this immovable God stand all His immovable believers, whose lives show the same inflexible rigidity, and who cannot move or dance under the weight of their heavy "faith." According to Stevens, when men worship this kind of God, they are simply absolutizing the one quality which they identify with existence. They are giving final expression to their belief that reality must be measured by the ideal of the indestructible atom or unyielding fact or ponderous stone.

For Stevens this understanding of reality is what makes men experience the modern city as a realm of intolerable pressure. It is not simply the outer conditions there, the congestion of people, or the concussion of events. It is also man's belief that static heaviness is the last and final law of existence. They see themselves held in the grip of some ponderous enormity, "society," perhaps, or "nature" or "God," and their own lives are molded accordingly.

> The solid was an age, a period
> With appropriate, largely English, furniture,

Barbers with charts of the only possible modes,
Cities that would not wash away in the mist,
Each man in his asylum maundering,
Policed by the hope of Christmas.[38]

When people bring this conception of reality to the modern
city, life there becomes unbearable.

What Stevens celebrates everywhere in his poetry is a redemption from this conception. He is convinced that all men wish
to live in a radiance of ever fresh transformations, in an atmosphere of dazzling and inexhaustible change. This is exactly what
awaits them in the engulfing moments. There reality discloses
itself to be not solid and heavy, but inconceivably light. It does
not push against the mind with pressure, not because it with-
holds its presence, but because at its very essence it is nothing
but a verve, an airy vivacity, a lightness of grace and change.
When it fills things, they lose every trace of heaviness. They
do not become less real, but differently real, real with surprising transformations instead of static permanence. They are
pervaded for an instant by this major reality, by this *vif*, this
dizzle-dazzle, this "imprescriptible zenith," this air of freshness,
clearness, greenness, blueness.[39]

Because this radiance appears under the most varied circumstances, because no objective heaviness or confusion can keep
it from happening when and as it will, and because in its presence all solid reality is completely dissolved away, Stevens can
see it as the true and final dimension of being, as the meta-
physically ultimate. The solid is not the *real* world at all; it is
simply an empty world, a husk waiting to be filled again with
glory by major reality. For Stevens, this is the wisdom by which
men are freed from the brutal oppressiveness of the city. They
do not need to fly to the country. If they do not change their
metaphysics, the country will seem just as solidly objective and
alien as the city. They need only to be perpetually attentive to
the engulfing moments, in the assurance that as long as the sun
turns and the seasons change, there is no situation that can
separate them from this glory.

In this light we can understand how Stevens' "philosophic"

efforts form a proper and invaluable climax to what has pre-occupied him from the beginning. In fact, if he had not been willing to carry his exploration to this metaphysical level, if he had remained the painter of surface dazzle that we find in many of his early poems, we would have to call him a mere aesthete and an escapist, a man who dabbles in odd experiences, not because they are authentic disclosures of reality, but because they distract and titillate his mind. But because of his willingness to see the engulfing moments as the genuine presence of reality and to follow out all the consequences of that perception, he is able to repudiate every kind of escapism. He now can say that the reality of the here and now is more wondrous than any creation of human fancy. He can do what neither Eliot nor Frost thought possible: he can write a *poetry of exaltation*. And he can do this without leaving the city, and without concocting some remote rural dream world or some remote religious heaven. The dazzling impact of the engulfing moment exalts the human spirit far beyond any joy it could ever reach by its own efforts. Even in the city, indeed, even in the midst of war and violence, the attentive mind is therefore able to find the world repeatedly transfigured by major reality. Even in such circumstances it will meet a flashing gaiety filling everything,

> So that morning and evening are like promises
>   kept,
> So that the approaching sun and its arrival,
> Its evening feast and the following festival,
>
> This faithfulness of reality, this mode,
> This tendance and venerable holding-in
> Make gay the hallucinations in surfaces.[40]

IX.

If the engulfing moments thus have a redemptive significance in Stevens' verse, they must be recognized and celebrated in human speech. Stevens is convinced that only a very special language can help us here. Only poetry with its images and rhythms, and only a poetry that has broken away from the static habits of prose and has become an artificial speech can faithfully recover this aspect of experience. Only poetry can catch the world freed from heaviness.

In this connection Stevens develops his theme that "poetry is a means of redemption," [41] that poetry is the better part of life,[42] that poetry is a cure of the mind. Both the philosopher and the religious man seek satisfaction for the human spirit in some remote elsewhere—in a cosmic absolute or in a supernatural heaven. Their language is completely unsuited to displaying the airy radiance in the here and now. Only poetic speech can catch the absolute where it really is, in the immediacy of the engulfing moment, in the honeycomb of the seeing eye. Stevens can therefore say that "poetry is a purging of the world's poverty and change and evil and death. It is a present perfecting, a satisfaction in the irremediable poverty of life." [43]

In the modern world, where so much misery arises from a false and one-sidedly objective experience of things, Stevens believes that the poet has a special role. He is the one who must "resist" the concussion of events, and free men from every kind of pressure. He is the one who must restore to them a new metaphysics, who must through his verbal poetry transmit to them a sense of the poetry of reality itself. He shows men how the sun comes bubbling up upon the business world and dissolves its ponderous projects. He prevents the eye from fixing things in static space, and the mind from escaping to remote abstractions. He discloses the permanent impermanence in which things roll, the sheen that covers them in the engulfing moments. His purpose is to show that the world for which men most desperately hunger is one that actually touches them every day. When a poet does this, Stevens observes, then

> how easy it is suddenly to believe in the poem as one has never believed in it before, suddenly to require of it a meaning beyond what its words can possibly say, a sound beyond any giving of the ear, a motion beyond our previous knowledge of feeling.[44]

X.

Insofar as this experience of the engulfing moment is converted into a deliberate world-view and made the norm by which to judge every reality and to redeem every human situation, the Christian community can only reject it. In that form it would deny that Christ alone is the revealer of God and the redeemer of men; it would identify these functions exclusively with the engulfing moment itself. It certainly appears that Stevens in his own life did adopt just such a world-view, and did completely repudiate the worship of God through Jesus Christ.

But for the act of reading Stevens' poetry, this question of a world-view is not involved. His eccentric style is poetically valid. It does not strike the ear as a vehicle for his personal philosophy, but as a rich recovery of an aspect of perceptual experience. In this respect his verse is more consistently disciplined than Robert Frost's. It is precisely the power of his poetry, however, that poses an important problem to the Christian community. It is the problem of nature and her glory.

For three centuries now, Christians have had to deal with that part of the world which science studies. Their custom has been to identify it with "God's creation." They have said that when God established a realm of creatures over against himself, what he produced was a system of identifiable objects, empirical facts, and repetitive events. He created the objective realm which confronts human experience and which science wants to understand. "God's creation," in other words, is just another name for what the physicists and biologists call "nature." Though borrowed originally from the deists, this idea became very widespread, because it enabled Christians to accept the work of science as dealing with a reality grounded and sustained by God himself. What could be more satisfactory! Scientists are given a religious reassurance about the reality of the phenomena they study, and Christians can enjoy every scientific discovery and technological conquest as a new appreciation of God's creation.

From another viewpoint, however, this development proved

to be disastrous. For it meant that Christians unwittingly committed themselves to the principle that existence depends on
having some kind of objective identity, of belonging to the
world "out there." It meant that God made things real by giving them solid, self-enclosed identities. It meant that God created only such things as can stand up under our most unflicker-
ing gaze and show their solidity. Any world that we might meet
in a dream or see under the spell of a momentary impression
was considered to have no real, God-given existence. It was
merely a product of our own minds. To take such a fancy seriously was to be "superstitious." That is, it was to be somehow
false to God as well as to scientific reason.

In this way, God was made to appear as the foundation for
all *stasis*. He was the one who gave everything that quota of
heaviness which it had to have in order to exist as a separate
entity. He was himself heaviness *par excellence*, and some of
the Germans even came to think of Him, not as the life, but as
the "ground" of this world. He established things in their predictable behavior and even-keeled routine. No disorder, no upheaval, no zoom or zing belonged to His domain. His creation
was good, and reflected His goodness, because it moved in such
settled ways. New possibilities arose gradually and "naturally,"
in strict conformity with what had always been the case. Radical
and staggering novelty was simply not part of the divine character. Therefore men could be confident that once they gained
enough knowledge, nothing would ever happen, even from God,
to cause them surprise. To be God's creature meant to be set in
a divinely immobile stability. He was the author of an orderly,
rational, safe, and dull world.

The disaster here was not in any particular theological idea as
such, but in the atmosphere of static stability that had become
identified with God and with man's life with God. No one could
conceive of dancing or leaping in this God's presence. Isaiah had
once said that they who wait for the Lord shall soar up with
wings like eagles, but such dynamic activity no longer seemed
appropriate. Bodily movement and even gay colors could not be
reconciled with this God. People *sat* before Him in church, just

as the universe sat before Him in its material stability. Each worshiping individual was bound within his own unchangeable identity and held to the benches by the suffocating weight of reverence. The church services reflected the heaviness that had become God's mark. Even "faith" came to mean a rigid submission to certain inflexible truths, and "peace" meant the security of an immovable assurance.

Perhaps nowhere did this atmosphere have a more pernicious influence than upon the Christian picture of heaven. Since the eighteenth century, this has not been thought of primarily as a *life*, full of joy and feasting, of vital play and dazzling surprise. It has become a static place, where ponderous choirs roar on endlessly and sobriety freezes the human spirit. Stasis, always stasis—that has to be the condition for heavenly existence, since it is the condition of God. Rupert Brooke caught the ugly oppressiveness of this kind of heaven in his poem "Song of the Children in Heaven" (1907).

> And when on whistles and toy drums
> We make a loud amusing noise,
> Some large official seraph comes
> And scolds, and takes away our toys,
> Bids us sit still and be good boys.
>
> And when a baby laughs up here
> Or rolls his crown about in play,
> There is a pause. God looks severe;
> The Angels frown, and sigh and pray,
> And some-one takes the crown away.

This ideal of a one-sidedly static heaven actually represents hell for certain aspects of human nature. Men have their vitality and imaginative needs. They want to be enchanted as well as preserved. They want glory, and not just solid endurance. We need not be surprised that by the turn of this century many Christians had excluded the hope of heaven from their own religion, and were nourishing their Christian motivation with the dynamic problems of social justice. This picture of heaven was, however, only one instance of the anti-imaginative, anti-vital ideal of objective solidity with which the whole Christian life had become saddled. Needless to say, this Christian orientation felt deeply threatened by modern art, with its seething dynamism and its passion for breaking apart static forms.

Stevens' poetry cuts to the root of this whole static atmosphere. For he elucidates a dimension of concrete perceptual experience in which nature is not "out there," and things do not appear as self-enclosed objects. This nature is a realm of perpetual transformation and startling surprise. It has a kind of glory. There is nothing which requires the Christian to fear what is unstable, and to make God the antidote for that particular fear. There is nothing in the Bible or the creeds or the church fathers that identifies God's creation with an objective world of static entities, nothing which says that reality is known better by a long stare than by a dream or a momentary impression. All this is merely the bias of one type of human personality, which craves ordered security and does not like to be dismayed with surprise. It is certainly a legitimate bias, but hardly an absolute norm for portraying the nature and goodness of God.

What the Bible and the church fathers do make clear about the world of God's creation is that it is a glorified world. It is not nature as we now see it, a realm of solid facts and repetitive processes. It is a reality irradiated everywhere by the splendor of the divine glory. It is a reality that men shall know only at the consummation of history, when God's glory will fill all things. There were no grounds, therefore, for identifying what God created with the stable nature investigated by science and cherished by common sense. When this world is actually revealed as God's creation, it will stagger the imagination. It will certainly not be cut down to the shape of what men find normal.

If we keep the thought of glory in mind, then the enjoyment of Stevens' poetry becomes a very valuable experience for the Christian community. In this age of anxiety and violence, glory is out of fashion, even in the churches. Men need to recover a sense of the glory of nature, if only to have it constantly overcome by their sense of the glory of God. They also need a *lan-*

guage of exaltation, an artificial language. Stevens' poetic diction reminds them that such a language cannot be found in ordinary speech.

NOTES FOR CHAPTER FOUR

1. Wallace Stevens' complete works are contained in three volumes, cited below, all published by Alfred A. Knopf, Inc.

2. *The Collected Poems of Wallace Stevens* (New York: Alfred A. Knopf, Inc., 1954), p. 121.

3. *Ibid.*, pp. 349f.

4. See *ibid.*, p. 365.

5. See *ibid.*, p. 228.

6. See *ibid.*, p. 237.

7. *Ibid.*, p. 302.

8. See John Locke, *Essay Concerning Human Understanding* (1890), II, chap. viii, p. 9.

9. Joseph Addison, *The Spectator*, No. 413.

10. *The Collected Poems . . .* , p. 398.

11. *Ibid.*, p. 288.

12. See *ibid.*, p. 448.

13. See *ibid.*, p. 228.

14. See Wallace Stevens, *Opus Posthumous*, ed. Samuel French Morse (New York: Alfred A. Knopf, Inc., 1957), p. 116.

15. See *ibid.*, p. 110.

16. See *The Collected Poems . . .* , p. 270.

17. *Ibid.*, p. 441.

18. *Ibid.*, p. 371.

19. *Opus Posthumous*, p. 160.

20. Marguerite Wilkinson, *New Voices, An Introduction to Contemporary Poetry* (Rev. ed.; New York: The Macmillan Company, 1921), pp. 85ff.

21. *Opus Posthumous*, p. 161.

22. *The Collected Poems . . .* , p. 514.

23. *Ibid.*, p. 224.

24. *Ibid.*, p. 481.

25. Leo Stein, *Appreciation: Painting, Poetry and Prose* (New York: Crown Publishers, Inc., 1947), pp. 103f.

26. See *Opus Posthumous*, pp. 158, 173.

27. *The Collected Poems . . .* , p. 347.

28. *Ibid.*, p. 205.

29. *Opus Posthumous*, p. 213.

30. See *The Collected Poems . . .* , p. 533.

31. *Ibid.*, p. 444.
32. *Ibid.*, p. 508.
33. *Ibid.*, p. 373.
34. *Opus Posthumous*, p. 169.
35. *Ibid.*, p. 164.
36. Wallace Stevens, *The Necessary Angel, Essays on Reality and the Imagination* (New York: Alfred A. Knopf, Inc., 1951), p. 18.
37. *Ibid.*, pp. 13–27.
38. *Opus Posthumous*, p. 68.
39. See *The Collected Poems* . . . , pp. 459, 530.
40. *Ibid.*, p. 472.
41. *Opus Posthumous*, p. 160.
42. See *Ibid.*, p. 158.
43. *Ibid.*, p. 167.
44. *Ibid.*, p. 210.

Chapter Five

Against Spiritual Pride

THE THREE POETS whom I have examined all belong to the same literary generation. They published their first books of poetry within a decade of each other (Frost in 1913, Eliot in 1917, and Stevens in 1923). They were the ones who had to break free from the dreamy, let's-escape-to-the-woods kind of verse that had been the fashion. They had to face the urbanization of modern life, not so much as a social phenomenon, but as a domain of immediate experience that molded the sounds and rhythms of living speech.

I have studied these poets, however, not because of their similarities, but because of their differences, because of the striking variety of poetic styles that they developed even as members of the same generation. Think of the contrast between the jangle of voices in Eliot's lines and Frost's rural tranquility; or between these conversational tones and Stevens' artificiality. Each of these men perfected a verbal music of his own, and thereby brought a different aspect of immediate experience into focus. Eliot clarified the levels of pain with which the city grates against the human consciousness. Frost celebrated the concrete integrity of individual things. Stevens explored the fugitive effect of sunlight and weather, those self-obliterating moments when everything seems filled by a queer immensity.

I have indicated how each of these styles has a specific value for members of the Christian community. It may point up the new patterns in everyday speech. Or it may confront Christians with some aspect of experience that they have been systematically ignoring. At the same time, I have tried to show that there is no direct "Christian" meaning to be found in these poets. Their work does not have value because of what they "believe" or do not "believe," because they possess some kind of "world-view," or because they have been able to break free from the "scientific picture of things," or because they offer a good diagnosis of "modern man's predicament." Their works are significant for the Christian community at the same level as they are for everyone else—as experiments with the music of words, as achievements of poetry. The poems of Eliot or Frost or Stevens have value for the Christian provided he submits to their spell; provided he does not try to be self-consciously religious, but lets their metaphors and rhythms sink into his imagination and give satisfying form to some aspect of immediate experience.

The real enemy of poetry within the Christian community is not the love of God, but the pride of men who want to be superior to the "ordinary" world and closed off from the risks and shames of the ongoing life. It is the kind of religious pride represented in the New Testament by the Pharisee. Today it often shows itself in what might be called "viewpoint Christianity." For some time now Christians have been absorbed in defining and defending what they believe against their own rival groups and against various secular ideologies. In the process there has been a tendency to identify the Christian life with clinging to certain given truths, rather than with being carried by God's grace into a continually redemptive engagement with the world. Being a Christian has come to mean possessing a self-conscious set of beliefs, a viewpoint. A Christian is someone who is closed, rather than open, to the shock of daily experience. He is supposed to have the answers. When confronted by a situation, he presumably withdraws into his treasure house of truth, puts on the right Christian principles, and then returns to the world ready for action. He is the man who does not dare touch any situation or enter into any relationship or have any experience until he has first interpreted and disinfected it with his Christian viewpoint.

Poetry provides a constant help against this closed-off, self-secure kind of Christianity. It reminds the Christian that he, like everyone else, lives in a dynamic and swift-moving interaction with the concrete world, an interaction too complex for him even to recognize, much less control. It shows him how little his consciously arranged beliefs sometimes play in his own immediate existence, how greatly he deceives himself with spiritual pride in pretending that he lives withdrawn from the world, and how much every moment of his life depends, not on his own deliberate convictions, but on the free and inscrutable workings of God's grace in his concrete experience.

To be sure, things in their immediate impact may distract a person with their dazzle and specious vitality. They may lead him to forget God. But the antidote to this distraction is not to run away from immediate experience, but to bite into it more deeply, until its limitations and deficiencies burn on the tongue. After all, Christ did not overcome death by believing in a doctrine of resurrection, but by entering into death and concretely discovering its limits. Having established this way, he calls men to follow him there. If a person ceases to be enchanted by worldly things, this is not because he has withdrawn from the world or has made himself believe harder in some safe, authorized doctrine, but because he has perceived the emptiness of the world concretely. He has moved at the same level as Frost does, for instance, in his poem "Nothing Gold Can Stay."

> Nature's first green is gold,
> Her hardest hue to hold.
> Her early leaf's a flower;
> But only so an hour.
> Then leaf subsides to leaf.
> So Eden sank to grief,
> So dawn goes down to day.
> Nothing gold can stay.

A Christian who believes that men are saved from the deceptions and evils of this world by some kind of spiritual withdrawal or by encasing themselves in a set of self-conscious beliefs is actually repudiating the flesh of Christ. He is saying that in

Christ God has not made this concrete world the region of His grace and victory. But this is exactly what God has done, according to the testimony of Christ's life and death, according to the witness of the Christian sacraments, and according to ongoing service of Christian charity to man's fleshly needs.

Poetry is therefore valuable to the Christian community insofar as it is not self-consciously religious, insofar as it does not withdraw to some spiritual plateau or try to propagate the Christian viewpoint, insofar as it continues to be a language of rhythm and metaphor, and thus to celebrate the perceptual life of the flesh.

HADDAM HOUSE is the imprint of an editorial venture in the area of religious literature, which grew originally out of the common concerns of The Edward T. Hazen Foundation, the Young Men's Christian Association, and the Young Women's Christian Association. It signifies books that deal with the moral and religious questions of students and other young people, although many HADDAM HOUSE books appeal to a wider audience, including the leaders and teachers of youth.

Through an Editorial Advisory Committee, the publisher studies the changing needs for religious literature, plans books, and seeks as authors not only experienced writers but new voices qualified to give fresh guidance to young men and women in these days. The present membership of the Editorial Advisory Committee includes: Richard T. Baker, *Chairman*, David Byers, Wayne Cowan, Virginia Corwin, John Maguire, John Oliver Nelson, and Jean M. Whittet.

See the following pages for an up-to-date list of HADDAM HOUSE books in print.

HADDAM HOUSE BOOKS

Primer for Protestants — James Hastings Nichols

Youth Asks About Religion — Jack Finegan

The Human Venture in Sex, Love, and Marriage — Peter A. Bertocci

Rediscovering the Bible — Bernhard W. Anderson

The Unfolding Drama of the Bible — Bernhard W. Anderson

The Student Prayerbook — John Oliver Nelson and Others, Editors

Community of Faith — T. Ralph Morton

Politics for Christians — William Muehl

The Paradoxes of Democracy — Kermit Eby and June Greenlief

The Tragic Vision and the Christian Faith — Nathan A. Scott, Editor

Conscience on Campus — Waldo Beach

The Prophetic Voice in Modern Fiction — William R. Mueller

The Renewal of Hope — Howard Clark Kee

Christianity and Communism Today — John C. Bennett

The Christian as a Doctor — James T. Stephens and Edward LeRoy Long, Jr.

Christianity and the Scientist — Ian G. Barbour

The Art of Christian Doubt — Fred Denbeaux

The Christian as a Journalist — Richard T. Baker

Taking the Bible Seriously — Leander E. Keck

Exploring the Logic of Faith — Kent Bendall and Frederick Ferre

The Recovery of Life's Meaning — W. Paul Jones

The Christian as a Businessman — Harold L. Johnson

The Celebration of Flesh — Arthur C. McGill